Chapter 1: Defining the Role of an IT Manager

As technology continues to evolve and play an increasingly crucial role in business operations, the demand for skilled IT managers has also risen. In today's dynamic and tech-driven workplace, the IT manager serves as a vital link between technology and the business, ensuring that the organization's technological needs are met while aligning with its overall goals and objectives. This chapter will delve into the intricacies of the role of an IT manager, including responsibilities, qualities, and skills needed to excel in this position.

Defining the Role

The role of an IT manager can vary depending on the organization's size, industry, and specific needs. However, the core responsibilities of an IT manager revolve around leading and directing the organization's information technology initiatives, strategies, and operations. The IT manager is responsible for overseeing the technology infrastructure, managing IT teams, ensuring compliance with industry regulations, budgetary management, and driving innovation within the organization.

Responsibilities

The responsibilities of an IT manager encompass a wide range of tasks that are vital to the smooth functioning of an organization. One of the primary responsibilities is managing the organization's IT projects. This involves developing project plans, allocating resources, monitoring progress, and ensuring timely completion of projects within budget. Additionally, the IT manager is responsible for implementing and maintaining IT policies and procedures, ensuring data security and protection against cyber threats, and managing vendor relationships. Communication is also a significant responsibility of an IT manager. They serve as a liaison between the IT department and other business units, ensuring that technology aligns with the organization's overall goals and objectives. Effective communication is essential for managing expectations, providing updates on IT initiatives, and understanding the needs of various stakeholders.

Another crucial responsibility of an IT manager is managing the IT team. This involves recruitment, training, and performance management, as well as fostering a collaborative and innovative culture within the team. The IT manager is also responsible for staying up-to-date with the latest technology trends, assessing their potential impact on the organization, and making strategic recommendations.

Qualities and Skills Needed

Being an IT manager requires a unique combination of technical expertise, leadership skills, and business acumen. The ideal IT manager possesses a deep understanding of technology trends and tools, along with the ability to communicate complex technical concepts in a clear and concise manner. They should also possess strong project management skills and the ability to handle multiple projects simultaneously while adhering to timelines and budgetary constraints. To excel in this role, an IT manager must also possess excellent leadership skills, including effective communication, decision-making, and problem-solving abilities. They should have the ability to build and lead high-performing teams and foster a collaborative and positive work environment. Business acumen is also a crucial quality for an IT manager, as they are responsible for aligning technology initiatives with the organization's overall goals and objectives. In terms of technical skills, an IT manager should have a solid understanding of technology infrastructure, including hardware, software, networks, and security. They should also have experience with project management methodologies and tools, as well as experience in budgeting and resource management.

In conclusion, the role of an IT manager is critical to the success of an organization's technological initiatives. It requires a unique combination of technical expertise, leadership skills, and business acumen. As technology continues to advance, the role of an IT manager will become increasingly vital in driving innovation and growth within organizations. In the following chapters, we will delve deeper into the critical responsibilities and skills needed to be a successful IT manager.

Chapter 2: Setting Objectives and Creating a Roadmap - Establishing Goals, Short-Term and Long-Term Planning

As an IT manager, it is vital to have a clear vision and objectives for your department. Setting goals and creating a roadmap is crucial for the success of any organization. In this chapter, we will discuss the importance of establishing goals, short-term and long-term planning, and creating a roadmap for your IT team.

Establishing Goals

Establishing goals is the first step towards building a successful IT team. Goals provide a sense of direction, motivation, and focus for your team. They help you define what you want to achieve and create a clear path towards achieving it. When setting goals, it is essential to keep them SMART – Specific, Measurable, Achievable, Relevant, and Time-bound. Specific goals define precisely what you want to achieve. Measurable goals have specific metrics that can be used to track progress. Achievable goals are realistic and attainable. Relevant goals align with the overall objectives of the organization. And time-bound goals have a clear deadline for completion. As an IT manager, you should involve your team in the goal-setting process. This will help create a sense of ownership and accountability within the team. Engage your team in discussions to identify the goals that are most important to them and how they can contribute to achieving them.

Short-Term and Long-Term Planning

Short-term planning involves creating a roadmap that outlines the steps needed to achieve your goals within a specific timeframe, usually less than one year. It focuses on day-to-day operations and immediate goals that need to be accomplished. Long-term planning, on the other hand, involves looking at the bigger picture and setting goals and objectives for the next three to five years. It takes into consideration the organization's vision and how the IT department can align with it to achieve long-term success. For short-term planning, it is essential to prioritize tasks and allocate resources accordingly. This will ensure that your team stays on track and meets deadlines. Use project management tools to plan, track and monitor progress in real-time.

Long-term planning requires a strategic approach. It involves looking at the organization's objectives and identifying where the IT department can contribute. This includes anticipating future technology trends and how they can be leveraged to improve the organization's operations.

Creating a Roadmap

Creating a roadmap involves combining short-term and long-term planning to create a clear path towards achieving your goals. It is a visual representation of your goals, plans, and strategies. A roadmap provides visibility and transparency to your team and stakeholders into the IT department's priorities and how they align with the organization's objectives. When creating a roadmap, it is crucial to have a realistic timeline and to involve your team in the process. This will ensure that the roadmap is achievable and that everyone is on the same page. A roadmap should also be flexible to accommodate any changes or unexpected events. A roadmap should also include specific milestones and deadlines for each goal. This will help your team stay focused and motivated to achieve them. It should also highlight any dependencies between tasks to ensure that everything is aligned and nothing falls through the cracks.

In conclusion, setting objectives and creating a roadmap is essential for any successful IT manager. It provides direction, motivation, and focus for your team, and ensures that the IT department is aligned with the organization's vision. Remember to involve your team in the goal-setting and planning processes, and to keep your goals SMART. With a well-defined roadmap, your team will be on the path to achieving great success.

Chapter 3: Building and Managing a High-Performing IT Team

Hiring the Right Team Members

Building a high-performing IT team starts with hiring the right individuals. As an IT manager, it is your responsibility to not only find candidates with the necessary technical skills, but also those who align with your team's values and goals. The key is to look beyond just their qualifications on paper and assess their overall personality and cultural fit within your team. In today's highly competitive market, it can be easy to get caught up in the race for candidates with impressive resumes and extensive experience. However, it's important to remember that skills can be taught and developed, but character and personality are innate. Look for candidates who display not only technical competency, but also a strong work ethic, positive attitude, and willingness to learn and adapt.

You can also consider incorporating behavioral and personality assessments into your hiring process. These can provide valuable insights into a candidate's communication style, level of motivation, and working preferences. This can help you determine if they will be a good fit for your team and organization.

Developing Skills and Knowledge

Once you have assembled your team, it is important to focus on their continued development and growth. As technology is constantly evolving, it is crucial for IT professionals to stay updated with the latest trends and advancements. As an IT manager, you can provide opportunities for your team to develop their skills and knowledge through various means such as training programs, conferences, and workshops. Additionally, creating a culture of learning and continuous improvement within your team can also be beneficial. Encourage your team to share their knowledge and learn from each other. This not only helps in building a stronger team dynamic, but also allows for cross-training and knowledge transfer.

Investing in your team's development not only benefits them, but also your organization as a whole. You will have a team of highly skilled and knowledgeable individuals who are capable of tackling any challenges that may arise.

Team Motivation

Motivation is a key factor in building and maintaining a high-performing IT team. As an IT manager, it is your task to keep your team motivated and engaged. This can be a challenging task, especially in a fast-paced and often stressful IT environment. However, with the right tools and techniques, you can create a work culture that fosters motivation and encourages your team to reach their full potential. One effective way to boost motivation is by recognizing and celebrating team achievements. Not only does this make your team feel valued and appreciated, but also encourages healthy competition and teamwork. It is important to also provide regular feedback and acknowledge individual contributions. This not only boosts motivation, but also allows for areas of improvement to be identified and addressed. Another important aspect of motivation is creating a positive work culture. This includes promoting work-life balance, fostering open communication, and providing opportunities for personal and professional growth. A happy and motivated team is essential for maintaining productivity and achieving success.

In conclusion, building and managing a high-performing IT team requires a combination of strategic hiring, continuous development, and effective motivation techniques. With the right approach and mindset, you can create a team that is not only capable and skilled, but also passionate and motivated to achieve success. As an IT manager, it is your responsibility to cultivate a culture of excellence within your team and continually strive towards reaching new heights.

Chapter 4: Communication Strategies for Effective IT Management

Communication Styles

As an IT manager, effective communication is crucial to your success. In order to lead and manage your team effectively, you must be able to communicate clearly and efficiently with them. But not everyone communicates in the same way, and as an IT manager, it is important for you to adapt your communication style based on the situation and the individual you are speaking to.

Understanding the different communication styles is the first step towards effective communication. There are four main styles of communication - assertive, aggressive, passive, and passive-aggressive. Each style has its own strengths and weaknesses, and as an IT manager, you must be able to identify and utilize the most appropriate style for the given situation.

Building Rapport

Building rapport with your team is essential in creating a productive and positive work environment. Rapport is the bond and trust that is established between individuals, and it is the foundation for effective communication and teamwork. To build rapport with your team, it is important to show genuine interest and respect for each team member. Take the time to get to know your team on a personal level, such as their interests, values, and goals. This will not only strengthen your relationship with your team, but it will also enable you to understand their communication style and adapt accordingly. Actively listening is another crucial aspect of building rapport. Listen to your team members' concerns, ideas, and suggestions without judgment or interruption. This will make them feel heard and valued, and they will be more likely to open up and communicate freely with you.

Handling Conflicts

Managing conflicts is a part of any managerial position, and as an IT manager, it is important for you to handle conflicts professionally and effectively. Conflicts are inevitable in a high-stress and fast-paced environment like IT, but how you handle them can make all the difference in maintaining a positive and cohesive team. The first step in managing conflicts is to remain calm and composed. Take a step back and assess the situation objectively before reacting. It is important to address conflicts in a timely manner and not let them escalate. Communication is key in handling conflicts. Encourage open and honest communication between the conflicting parties. Act as a mediator and facilitate a conversation where both sides can express their concerns and work towards a solution. It is essential to listen to both sides and consider their perspective while finding a resolution. As an IT manager, it is also important to set ground rules and expectations for how conflicts should be handled within the team. This will prevent conflicts from arising in the first place and provide a framework for resolving them if they do occur.

In conclusion, effective communication is an essential skill for IT managers. Understanding different communication styles, building rapport with your team, and handling conflicts professionally are all key elements in mastering communication as an IT manager. By utilizing these strategies, you can create a positive and cohesive team that will help drive your IT projects towards success.

Chapter 5: Creating and Managing Budgets for Optimal Resource Management and Cost Reduction Strategies

Creating and Managing Budgets

Managing the budget is a crucial aspect of being an IT manager. It requires a delicate balance between managing expenses and investing in tools and resources that will drive growth and efficiency for the organization. As an IT manager, you must be able to understand and communicate the financial implications of IT decisions to stakeholders, while also ensuring that the IT department stays within the allocated budget. One of the first steps in creating a budget is to review the previous year's budget and expenditure. This analysis will help you identify any overspending and areas where you can make adjustments. You should also consult with other departments and stakeholders to understand their IT needs and budget limitations. This information will assist you in developing a realistic budget that takes into account all necessary IT expenditures and aligns with the organization's overall financial goals.

Optimizing Resources

In today's fast-paced business landscape, it is essential to optimize resources to stay ahead of the competition. As an IT manager, it is your responsibility to ensure that the organization's IT resources are utilized efficiently and effectively. This requires effectively managing the IT team and identifying areas where resources can be optimized to increase productivity and reduce costs. One effective strategy is to implement a resource tracking system that can monitor the utilization of hardware, software, and personnel. This data can help you identify underutilized resources, leading to potential cost savings. It also allows you to reallocate resources to match demand and address any skill gaps within the team. Additionally, implementing technology tools, such as automation and cloud computing, can help optimize resources and reduce costs in the long run.

Cost Reduction Strategies

Cost reduction is an essential aspect of budget management for any organization. As an IT manager, you have a crucial role in driving cost reductions within the IT department. This requires identifying areas where costs can be minimized without negatively impacting the quality of services provided.

One cost reduction strategy is to negotiate with vendors and suppliers for better deals or discounts. By leveraging the organization's purchasing power, you may be able to secure more favorable pricing for hardware, software, and services. Another strategy is to implement cost-efficient solutions, such as open-source software, instead of expensive proprietary options. Additionally, regularly reviewing and optimizing IT processes can help identify areas where costs can be reduced without compromising efficiency.

Incorporating Cost Reduction in Decision Making

As an IT manager, it is crucial to consider cost implications in every IT decision you make. Any new project or investment must align with the organization's financial goals and stay within the allocated budget. Conduct a cost-benefit analysis for all proposed IT projects to determine the potential return on investment and the impact on the budget. This analysis should also include any long-term maintenance costs associated with the project. Furthermore, it is essential to communicate the cost implications with stakeholders and management before any decisions are made. This will help set expectations and prevent any budget surprises down the line. Regularly reviewing and providing updates on the budget to stakeholders will promote transparency and accountability within the IT department and the organization as a whole.

Conclusion

Managing budgets, optimizing resources, and implementing cost reduction strategies are critical responsibilities for an IT manager. By effectively managing the budget and making strategic decisions that align with the organization's financial goals, you will not only ensure the success of IT operations but also contribute to the overall growth and success of the organization. Remember to regularly review and adapt these strategies to align with the ever-changing needs of the organization. By continuously striving for efficiency and cost-effectiveness, you will be a valuable asset to the organization as the IT manager.

.

Chapter 6: Project Management for IT Managers

Project Planning and Execution: A Work of Art

As an IT manager, your role involves overseeing and leading various projects to ensure they are executed successfully. This requires a careful balance of technical expertise and project management skills. In this chapter, we will explore the art of project planning and execution and how you can master it as an IT manager.

Risk Management: Embracing the Unknown

Every project comes with its own set of risks, and as an IT manager, it is your responsibility to identify and manage them effectively. However, risk management is not just about avoiding potential problems - it is also about embracing the unknown and taking calculated risks that can lead to great success. In this section, we will delve into the world of risk management and how to use it to drive your projects towards success.

Managing Deadlines: A Symphony of Time Management

As an IT manager, you are often faced with tight deadlines and a multitude of tasks to complete within a given timeframe. It can sometimes feel like a never-ending symphony of time management, with each task requiring a specific note to be played at just the right time. In this section, we will explore the strategies and techniques you can use to effectively manage deadlines and keep your projects moving forward in a harmonious rhythm.

The Art of Project Planning and Execution

Project planning and execution is a delicate balance of skill, creativity, and strategic thinking. It is not just about creating a detailed plan and following it blindly. Instead, it is about using your expertise and experience to create a well-organized and actionable plan that takes into consideration all aspects of the project, including resources, budget, risks, and timelines. To start, it is crucial to have a clear understanding of the project objectives and deliverables. This will help you determine the scope of the project and establish a realistic timeline for completion. With this in mind, you can start breaking down the project into smaller, manageable tasks and assign them to your team members based on their strengths and expertise. Communication plays a vital role in project planning and execution. It is essential to keep all stakeholders informed and updated throughout the project, from the initial planning stages to the final delivery. This will help avoid miscommunication and ensure everyone is on the same page. Another critical aspect of project planning and execution is managing resources effectively. This includes not only the team members but also any external resources, such as vendors or contractors. As an IT manager, it is your responsibility to ensure that all resources are utilized efficiently and to make any adjustments as needed to keep the project on track.

The Balance of Risk Management

Risk management is often seen as a negative aspect of project management, as it involves identifying potential problems and finding ways to mitigate them. However, there is a positive side to risk management. By embracing the unknown and taking calculated risks, you can open up new opportunities and drive your project towards success. To effectively manage risks, it is crucial to have a detailed risk management plan in place. This involves identifying potential risks, assessing their impact and likelihood, and developing a plan to mitigate or address them. It is essential to involve your team and stakeholders in this process to ensure all perspectives are considered. In addition to managing potential risks, it is also essential to monitor and address any unforeseen risks that may arise during the project. This requires flexibility and adaptability, as well as effective communication with all stakeholders.

The Symphony of Time Management

Managing deadlines is a crucial aspect of project management, and it requires a good understanding of time management principles. To effectively manage deadlines, it is crucial to prioritize tasks and allocate time accordingly. This involves breaking down deadlines into smaller, manageable segments and working towards meeting each one. One helpful technique for managing deadlines is the Pomodoro method, where you work on a task for a set time period, usually 25 minutes, and then take a short break before returning to the task. This helps keep you focused and productive while also giving your brain a break. Communication is also essential when managing deadlines. It is crucial to keep stakeholders informed of progress and any changes to the timeline. If an unforeseen issue arises that may impact the deadline, it is important to communicate it as soon as possible and work together to find a solution.

In conclusion, project management for IT managers is a delicate balance of art and science. It involves creating a well-thought-out plan, embracing risk, and effectively managing time and resources. By mastering these skills, you can ensure the success of your projects and lead your team towards achieving their objectives.

Chapter 7: Policies, Procedures, and Compliance - Maintaining Order in IT Management

As an IT manager, one of your primary responsibilities is to ensure that your team operates within a set of established policies and procedures. These guidelines not only provide structure and direction for your team, but they also help to ensure the security and integrity of your organization's IT infrastructure. In this chapter, we will delve into the various aspects of creating, enforcing, and dealing with policy violations to effectively manage your IT operations.

Creating Policies and Procedures

Just like any other department in a company, the IT team must have clear and well-defined policies and procedures in place. These are essential to ensure that processes are executed correctly and consistently, and that the team is aligned with the overall goals and objectives of the organization. When creating policies and procedures, it is crucial to involve your team and other stakeholders. This not only helps to gain buy-in and support but also ensures that the policies are practical and attainable. Communicate the policies clearly and ensure that they are accessible to all team members. It is also advisable to review and update the policies periodically to reflect any changes in technology, processes, or industry standards.

Enforcing Compliance

Having policies and procedures in place is one thing, but enforcing compliance is another. As an IT manager, it is your responsibility to ensure that your team strictly adheres to the established guidelines. One way to achieve this is by incorporating them into your daily operations and processes.

Regular audits and checks can also help to identify any compliance gaps that need to be addressed. Depending on the severity of the violation, you may need to take disciplinary action, such as coaching or retraining. It is essential to handle policy violations consistently to maintain integrity and fairness within the team.

Dealing with Policy Violations

Even with clear policies and effective enforcement, policy violations can still occur. When this happens, it is important to handle the situation professionally and promptly. Start by gathering all the necessary information to understand the circumstances surrounding the violation. This may require reviewing policies, relevant documents, and speaking to the individuals involved.

Once you have all the information, approach the situation with empathy and professionalism. Communicate the violation clearly and discuss the consequences or next steps. It is important to address policy violations promptly to maintain the integrity and effectiveness of the policies.

In today's fast-paced and constantly evolving technology landscape, having a well-managed and structured IT team is crucial to the success of any organization. As an IT manager, it is your responsibility to establish and maintain policies and procedures that not only guide your team but also align with the goals and objectives of the organization. By creating clear policies, enforcing compliance, and addressing violations professionally, you can effectively manage your IT operations and maintain order within your team.

Chapter 8: Change Management and Leading Through Change

Understanding Change Management

Change is an inevitable aspect of any organization's growth and development. It can bring about new opportunities, improvements, and advancements, but it can also bring challenges and resistance. As an IT manager, it is your responsibility to understand the process of change management and how to lead your team through it effectively.

Change management involves the structured approach to transitioning individuals, teams, and organizations from the current state to a desired future state. It is a process that helps organizations assess, plan, implement, and monitor changes in a way that minimizes disruption and maximizes positive outcomes. And as an IT manager, you are responsible for managing change within your department and also helping your team members adapt to change.

Change Planning

Effective change management starts with proper planning. This involves understanding the reasons for the change, identifying the goals and objectives, and determining the necessary steps to implement the change. As an IT manager, you must work closely with your team and other stakeholders to create a detailed change plan that addresses all aspects of the change. The first step in change planning is to communicate the change to your team. This allows them to understand the reasons behind the change and how it will affect their work. It is important to address any concerns or questions they may have and involve them in the planning process. This will help to ensure their buy-in and cooperation during the change implementation.

Next, it is important to assess and identify potential risks and challenges that may arise during the change process. This allows you to anticipate and address any issues that may arise and mitigate their impact. It is also crucial to establish a timeline for the change and set realistic goals and milestones. This will help to keep the change process organized and on track.

Leading Through Change

As an IT manager, you are not just responsible for overseeing the change, but also for leading your team through it. Change can bring about uncertainty and discomfort for employees, and it is your role to guide and support them during this time. There are a few key strategies for effectively leading through change. Firstly, lead by example. It is important for you to embody the change and demonstrate a positive attitude towards it. This will encourage your team members to do the same and help them to feel more confident about the change. Communication is also crucial during change management. Keep your team members informed about the progress of the change and address any concerns or challenges that may arise. Be open and transparent with your communication and encourage your team members to do the same. Provide opportunities for feedback and input from your team members. This can help them feel involved and valued during the change process. It may also bring about valuable insights and suggestions for the change implementation. Lastly, remember to recognize and celebrate small wins and milestones during the change process. This will help to maintain motivation and morale within your team and keep them focused on the end goal.

In conclusion, change management is a critical skill for IT managers to master. By understanding the process of change management, properly planning for change, and effectively leading your team through it, you can ensure that changes are implemented successfully and positively impact your organization. As an IT manager, it is your responsibility to embrace change and help your team members do the same, ultimately leading your organization towards growth and success.

Chapter 9: IT Risk Management – Ensuring Secure and Efficient Operations

The role of an IT manager not only involves overseeing day-to-day operations, but also proactively identifying and addressing potential risks and threats to the organization's IT infrastructure. In today's digital age, where cyber attacks and data breaches are becoming increasingly prevalent, it is crucial for IT managers to be well-versed in risk management techniques to ensure the secure and efficient operations of their department. In this chapter, we will explore the key aspects of IT risk management, including identifying risks and threats, implementing security measures, and disaster recovery planning.

Identifying Risks and Threats

The first step in effective IT risk management is identifying potential risks and threats to the organization's IT infrastructure. This involves analyzing the organization's systems and processes, as well as external factors such as technological advancements and industry trends. IT managers must also stay updated on the latest cybersecurity threats and vulnerabilities to ensure timely risk identification and mitigation. One effective approach to identifying risks and threats is conducting a risk assessment. This involves a systematic evaluation of the potential risks and vulnerabilities within the organization's IT infrastructure. A risk assessment typically includes identifying critical assets, determining the likelihood and impact of potential risks, and assessing the existing security controls in place.

Another important aspect of identifying risks and threats is understanding the organization's risk appetite – the level of risk that the organization is willing to accept. This will help IT managers prioritize risks and allocate resources accordingly. For instance, a financial institution may have a lower risk appetite due to the sensitive nature of their data, while a retail organization may be more focused on risks related to customer data privacy.

Implementing Security Measures

Once the risks and threats have been identified, the next step is implementing security measures to prevent or mitigate their impact. This involves selecting and implementing appropriate security controls, such as firewalls, antivirus software, and intrusion detection systems. IT managers must carefully evaluate various security solutions and choose the ones that best fit the organization's needs and risk profile. In addition to implementing technical controls, IT managers also play a crucial role in establishing and enforcing security policies and procedures within the organization. This includes educating employees on best practices for data security and ensuring compliance with regulatory requirements.

Another important aspect of security measures is conducting regular security audits and assessments. This helps identify any vulnerabilities or weaknesses in the existing controls and allows for timely remediation. IT managers must also ensure that all security measures are regularly updated and patched to keep up with evolving threats.

Disaster Recovery Planning

Despite the best efforts to prevent security breaches, organizations must always be prepared for worst-case scenarios. Disaster recovery planning involves creating a comprehensive plan for how the organization will respond and recover from a major IT incident, such as a cyber attack or natural disaster. IT managers play a critical role in developing and implementing disaster recovery plans, which typically include:

- Creating backups of critical data and systems

- Developing a communication plan to keep stakeholders informed during an incident

- Identifying key personnel responsible for different aspects of the recovery process

- Establishing procedures for restoring systems and data

- Conducting regular drills and tests to ensure the plan is effective.

In today's interconnected world, disaster recovery planning must also consider potential disruptions from third-party vendors.

IT managers must work closely with vendors to ensure their disaster recovery plans align with the organization's own plans and requirements.

Conclusion

The key to effective IT risk management is a proactive and holistic approach that involves identifying, evaluating, and addressing potential risks and threats. IT managers must stay updated on the latest security trends and employ a combination of technical controls, policies and procedures, and disaster recovery planning to ensure the security and efficiency of their organization's IT operations. By following the techniques outlined in this chapter, IT managers can mitigate risks and ensure the continued success of their organization's IT department.

Chapter 10: Managing Vendors for IT Success: Selecting, Negotiating, and Evaluating Performance

As an IT manager, a large part of your job is working with external vendors to provide your organization with the necessary technology and services to support your business operations. Choosing the right vendors and managing those relationships effectively can greatly impact the overall success of your IT projects and the performance of your team. In this chapter, we will discuss the key aspects of selecting and managing vendors, negotiating contracts, and evaluating their performance.

Selecting and managing vendors

The process of selecting vendors should begin with a thorough evaluation of your organization's needs and the technology solutions required to meet them. It is essential to have a clear understanding of your project's requirements and objectives, including the specific features and functionality needed from a vendor. Once you have defined your expectations, you can start researching potential vendors to find the best fit for your organization. When evaluating vendors, it's crucial to look beyond their website and marketing materials. Dig deeper by requesting references from their current clients and checking online reviews to get a more realistic picture of their reputation and overall performance. You should also consider factors such as the vendor's experience, expertise in your industry, and their ability to provide ongoing support and maintenance. Additionally, consider the cost and value of the services they offer and ensure they fit within your allocated budget.

Once you have selected your vendors, it is vital to manage those relationships effectively. Communication is key to successful vendor management, and you should establish and maintain clear lines of communication to ensure that expectations and deliverables are clearly understood by both parties. It's also essential to have a dedicated point of contact within the vendor's organization for any issues or concerns that may arise.

Negotiating contracts

Contract negotiation is a crucial step in the vendor management process, and it's essential to approach it with a strategic mindset. Begin by defining the scope of work, timelines, and any other requirements that need to be included in the contract. It's also essential to identify any potential risks or issues that may arise and address them from the outset to avoid misunderstandings down the road. One of the most critical aspects of contract negotiation is establishing clear expectations and setting realistic performance metrics. These metrics will serve as a benchmark for measuring the vendor's performance, and they should be included in the contract along with consequences for not meeting them. This ensures that both parties are on the same page and provides a basis for holding the vendor accountable for their performance.

Furthermore, it's vital to carefully review the terms and conditions of the contract and negotiate any changes or additions that are necessary to protect your organization's interests. This includes items such as the termination clause, service level agreements, and confidentiality agreements. Be prepared to walk away from a vendor if they are not willing to negotiate terms that align with your needs and expectations.

Vendor performance evaluation

Measuring and evaluating a vendor's performance is a critical aspect of maintaining a successful relationship. It's essential to regularly review the vendor's performance against the agreed-upon metrics and address any issues that arise promptly. By monitoring performance closely, you can proactively address any problems before they escalate and ensure that your organization is getting the most value from their services. When evaluating a vendor's performance, it's essential to look beyond the metrics and consider the overall impact on your organization. Are they delivering on their promises, providing quality services, and being responsive to your needs? It's also essential to involve your team in the evaluation process, as they are in direct contact with the vendor and can provide valuable insights. In addition to evaluating their performance, it's crucial to maintain open communication with your vendors. Regular check-ins are an excellent way to stay informed of their progress and address any concerns or issues that may arise. By establishing a positive and collaborative relationship, you can work together with your vendors to achieve mutual success.

In conclusion, effectively managing vendors is a crucial aspect of being an IT manager. By defining your organization's needs and expectations, carefully selecting vendors, and negotiating contracts that align with your interests, you can build successful partnerships that drive innovation and growth. Consistently evaluating and communicating with your vendors will ensure that these relationships continue to support your organization's goals and deliver positive results.

Chapter 11: Implementing Quality Assurance for IT Projects

Quality assurance is crucial for any IT project, as it ensures that the final product or service meets the desired standards and expectations. As an IT manager, it is your responsibility to establish and maintain quality standards throughout the project lifecycle. In this chapter, we will discuss the key components of quality assurance and how you can implement them to ensure a successful IT project.

Establishing Quality Standards

The first step towards implementing quality assurance is to establish clear and measurable quality standards. This involves defining the desired quality for the project and identifying the key metrics that will be used to measure it. As an IT manager, it is important to involve all stakeholders in this process to ensure that their expectations are aligned with the project goals.

To establish effective quality standards, it is important to consider the specific requirements of the project and the expectations of the end-users. These standards should also be realistic and achievable within the given time and budget constraints. Additionally, you should also take into account any external quality standards that may be applicable to the project.

Conducting Quality Reviews

Once quality standards have been established, the next step is to conduct regular quality reviews throughout the project. This involves evaluating the project against the established standards and identifying any deviations or areas for improvement. Quality reviews can take various forms, such as code reviews, testing, and user feedback. It is important for IT managers to create a structured and transparent process for conducting quality reviews. This can involve setting up regular checkpoints and involving both the development team and end-users in the review process.

Additionally, it is important to document the outcomes of these reviews and take necessary corrective actions to ensure that project quality is maintained.

Continuous Improvement

Implementing quality assurance is an ongoing process and requires continuous effort to ensure that the project meets the desired standards. Therefore, it is important for IT managers to prioritize continuous improvement and foster a culture of learning within their teams. This can involve investing in training and development for team members, as well as implementing processes to capture and implement feedback from end-users. Continuous improvement can also involve adopting industry best practices and keeping up-to-date with the latest technologies and tools. As an IT manager, it is important to constantly evaluate and improve upon your own processes and strategies to ensure that your team is delivering high-quality products and services.

Conclusion

Establishing quality standards, conducting quality reviews, and prioritizing continuous improvement are essential components of successful quality assurance in IT projects. As an IT manager, it is your responsibility to ensure that these practices are implemented and followed throughout the project lifecycle to guarantee the delivery of a high-quality product or service. By involving all stakeholders, setting realistic standards, and fostering a culture of learning and improvement, you can ensure that your IT projects meet or even exceed expectations. In the next chapter, we will discuss the importance of IT asset management and how you can effectively manage your IT resources to support your projects.

Chapter 12: Managing IT Assets for Maximum Efficiency

Asset management is a crucial component of an IT manager's responsibilities. In today's fast-paced digital world, technology is constantly evolving, and organizations must keep up with the latest hardware and software to stay competitive. This requires IT managers to have a solid understanding of asset management principles and effectively manage the lifecycle of their IT assets. In this chapter, we will delve into the key aspects of managing IT assets and how to optimize their usage for maximum efficiency.

Managing Hardware and Software Assets

As an IT manager, you are responsible for ensuring that your organization's hardware and software assets are effectively managed. This means having a complete inventory of all assets, from computers and servers to operating systems and applications. This information is critical for decision-making purposes, such as equipment upgrades and budget planning. Having a comprehensive view of your assets also enables you to track their usage, ensuring that they are being utilized effectively and not sitting idle. With this data, you can make informed decisions on which assets need to be replaced, retired, or upgraded. Additionally, by having a complete list of assets, you can identify potential security risks or license violations.

Tracking and Managing Licenses

Managing licenses is a critical aspect of asset management, as it ensures that your organization is compliant with software usage agreements and avoids any legal repercussions. IT managers must have a system in place to track all software licenses and their expiry dates to avoid any potential legal or financial consequences.

Having a central repository for all license information can also help in identifying any unused or underutilized licenses that can be reassigned to other employees, eliminating the need for additional purchases. This proactive approach not only saves money but also keeps your organization's software usage in check.

Asset Lifecycle Management

Effective asset lifecycle management is essential for optimizing the usage of IT assets and reducing unnecessary expenses. It involves planning, acquiring, maintaining, and disposing of assets in a way that aligns with the organization's overall goals and objectives. Planning for asset lifecycle management involves determining the appropriate hardware and software needed to support the organization's operations. Acquiring assets requires careful evaluation of options, such as leasing versus buying, and selecting the best vendors for your organization's needs. Maintenance involves keeping assets up to date with the latest software updates and security patches, as well as ensuring regular maintenance and repairs to maximize the lifespan of assets. Disposing of assets often involves properly disposing of electronic waste and securely wiping any sensitive data from devices before disposal.

The Benefits of Effective Asset Management

With effective asset management, IT managers can reduce costs associated with asset ownership, minimize the risk of security breaches, and optimize technical resources. By truly understanding the organization's IT assets, managers can analyze their current and future needs to make informed decisions about asset investments and ensure optimal use of IT resources. Proper management of IT assets also leads to increased productivity and reduced downtime. With accurate tracking and maintenance, organizations can avoid disruption and delays caused by faulty or outdated equipment. This, in turn, leads to satisfied employees and customers, which ultimately contributes to the organization's success.

A Holistic Approach to IT Asset Management

To effectively manage IT assets, it is essential to have a holistic approach that encompasses hardware, software, and people. IT managers must not only manage physical assets but also ensure that employees have the necessary knowledge and skills to utilize them efficiently.

This can be achieved through implementing training programs and keeping employees updated on the latest technology and software updates. By empowering employees to make the most out of their IT assets, organizations can see a significant increase in productivity and overall performance.

Implementing an IT Asset Management System

Having a robust IT asset management system in place is crucial for IT managers to effectively manage their organization's assets. These systems provide a centralized platform for tracking all IT assets, their lifecycle, and other essential information such as software licenses, warranties, and maintenance schedules.

With an automated system, manual tracking and management of assets become a thing of the past, saving time and resources. These systems also come equipped with reporting capabilities, providing valuable insights on asset usage patterns and opportunities for cost savings.

In Conclusion

Effective management of IT assets is essential for any organization's success in today's digital landscape. By having a complete understanding of hardware and software assets and implementing an IT asset management system, IT managers can optimize assets' usage, reduce costs, and contribute to the organization's overall success. Remember, a holistic approach to asset management that includes employees is key to achieving maximum efficiency and productivity.

Chapter 13: Understanding Agile and DevOps: Implementing and Measuring Success

Understanding Agile and DevOps

When it comes to managing IT projects, traditional methodologies have often been cumbersome and time-consuming. In today's fast-paced digital landscape, businesses require a more streamlined and efficient approach to IT management. That's where Agile and DevOps come in. Agile and DevOps are two popular project management methodologies that have revolutionized the way IT projects are planned, executed, and delivered. While they have similarities, they also have distinct differences that set them apart. Understanding these differences is crucial for IT managers to determine which approach is best suited for their organization's needs. Agile is an iterative approach that focuses on delivering working software in short and frequent cycles, usually ranging from 2-4 weeks. It emphasizes continuous collaboration and feedback from the customer throughout the project. This allows for rapid adjustments and improvements to be made, ensuring that the final product meets the customer's expectations.

On the other hand, DevOps is a practice that emphasizes the collaboration between development (Dev) and operations (Ops) teams. It aims to bridge the gap between these two traditionally separate departments and create a culture of continuous integration and delivery. DevOps is all about automating processes, improving communication and collaboration, and ultimately delivering software faster and with fewer errors.

Implementing in an IT environment

The adoption of Agile and DevOps has been on the rise, especially in the IT industry. However, implementing these methodologies in an IT environment can be challenging. IT managers must have a clear understanding of their organization's current processes and the potential impact these methodologies will have when implemented. The first step in implementing Agile and DevOps is to ensure that all stakeholders, including the IT team, are on board. This involves educating them about the methodologies and the benefits they can bring. It is crucial to gain their buy-in and support to successfully implement any changes. Another key aspect of implementing Agile and DevOps in an IT environment is breaking down silos between development and operations teams. This can be achieved by fostering a culture of collaboration and communication, setting up agile teams, and implementing automated processes that facilitate continuous integration and delivery.

It is also essential to ensure that the organization's infrastructure is equipped to support Agile and DevOps practices. This may involve upgrading tools and technologies, providing necessary training to the IT team, and establishing metrics to measure success.

Measuring Success

One of the significant advantages of Agile and DevOps is the focus on continuous improvement. Therefore, measuring success is not only limited to the end product but also the processes and practices used throughout the project. For Agile, the success can be measured by the product's functionality and quality, customer satisfaction, and team productivity. On the other hand, DevOps success can be gauged by metrics such as deployment frequency, mean time to recover, and deployment success rate. It is also essential to measure the success of the cultural shift towards collaboration and continuous improvement. This can be done through regular team feedback, surveys, and tracking the number of issues raised and resolved.

In addition to these metrics, IT managers must also pay attention to financial metrics such as cost savings and return on investment. This will help justify the time and resources invested in implementing Agile and DevOps.

Conclusion

In conclusion, Agile and DevOps have proven to be beneficial for IT projects in terms of speed, efficiency, and customer satisfaction. However, the successful implementation of these methodologies requires a deep understanding of their principles, a commitment to cultural change within the organization, and the ability to measure success through various metrics. By embracing a more agile and collaborative approach, IT managers can master the strategies for success in today's fast-paced digital landscape.

Chapter 14: Embracing Technology: Staying Ahead in the Ever-Changing World of IT Management

Research and Learning: The Key to Success in the Fast-Paced IT Industry

In today's rapidly evolving world of technology, IT managers must constantly stay on top of the latest trends, tools and strategies to thrive in their role. This means dedicating time and resources towards research and learning, both for themselves and their team. One of the most effective ways to stay ahead of the game is to regularly attend industry conferences, workshops and seminars. These events offer a wealth of knowledge, insights and networking opportunities that can greatly benefit an IT manager's development. It's also important to allocate time for online research, where one can explore relevant blogs, articles and websites for valuable information and updates.

Additionally, encouraging a culture of continuous learning within the IT team can lead to a highly skilled and adaptable team that can keep up with the latest developments in the industry. This could involve organizing regular training sessions, providing access to online resources and encouraging team members to pursue certifications and professional development opportunities.

Incorporating New Technology: Maximizing the Potential of Innovative Tools

Technological advancements are happening at an unprecedented pace, and it's vital for IT managers to keep their finger on the pulse to identify new tools and techniques that can boost their team's performance. Embracing new technology can bring numerous benefits, from streamlining processes to improving communication and collaboration.

To successfully incorporate new technology, IT managers must first assess the needs of their team and organization. This involves identifying pain points, areas for improvement and goals that could be met with the help of innovative tools. From there, managers can research and test different options, select the most suitable ones and create a plan to implement them effectively. It's also essential to involve team members in the decision-making process and provide adequate training and support to ensure a smooth transition.

Staying Ahead of Industry Changes: The Importance of Proactive Adaptation

The IT industry is constantly changing, and it's crucial for IT managers to stay ahead of these changes to remain competitive. This requires a proactive approach to adapt to new technologies, business models and industry standards as they emerge. To stay ahead of industry changes, IT managers must keep their ear to the ground and monitor trends and developments. This could involve networking with peers, attending conferences and subscribing to industry newsletters. Another key aspect is to foster a culture of innovation and experimentation within the team. Encouraging team members to explore new technologies and ideas can lead to innovative solutions that keep the organization ahead of the curve.

Moreover, IT managers must be flexible and open-minded, willing to adapt their strategies and processes to accommodate new industry changes. This may require adjusting budget allocations, reallocating resources and revising project plans. But by doing so, IT managers can ensure their team is always on the cutting edge, providing the best services and solutions to their organization.

Final Thoughts

In the fast-paced world of IT management, research, learning and adaptation are crucial for success. By dedicating time and resources to stay informed about industry developments, implementing new technology effectively, and being proactive in adapting to changes, IT managers can lead their team and organization towards continuous growth and success.

Chapter 15: Setting and Measuring IT Service Levels: Ensuring Customer Satisfaction

Managing IT service levels is a crucial aspect of an IT manager's role. It involves setting service level agreements (SLAs), measuring and improving service levels, and monitoring customer satisfaction. In today's competitive business landscape, providing high-quality IT services is essential for success. As an IT manager, you are responsible for ensuring that your team delivers exceptional service to internal and external customers, and this chapter will guide you in doing just that.

Setting Service Level Agreements

Service level agreements are vital documents that outline the responsibilities, expectations, and standards for IT services provided to users. These agreements need to be agreed upon by both the IT department and the customers. They act as a contract between the two parties and serve as a baseline for measuring service levels. As an IT manager, it is crucial to establish clear and measurable SLAs to ensure that your team meets customer expectations and stays on track. When creating SLAs, it is essential to involve your team and understand the capabilities and limitations of your IT infrastructure. This will help in setting realistic and achievable service level targets. It is also crucial to consider the different types of services provided, such as infrastructure, applications, and support, and set specific SLAs for each.

Additionally, SLAs should be periodically reviewed and updated to reflect changes in technology or business needs. As an IT manager, you need to have open communication with your customers to ensure their needs are met and SLAs are revised accordingly.

Measuring and Improving Service Levels

Once SLAs are in place, the next step is to measure and improve service levels continuously. This requires tracking service metrics and analyzing data to identify areas for improvement. Common metrics used for measuring service levels include response time, resolution time, downtime, and customer satisfaction. Analyzing these metrics can help identify patterns and areas of improvement. For example, if there is a recurring issue with a particular application causing prolonged downtime, steps can be taken to improve its stability. It is crucial to involve your team in this process as they have a better understanding of the technical aspects and can suggest solutions to improve service levels.

In addition to analyzing data, regular performance reviews with your team are vital for improving service levels. These reviews should be used to identify any roadblocks or areas for improvement and come up with action plans to address them. Encouraging a culture of continuous improvement in your team will help in delivering high-quality services consistently.

Monitoring Customer Satisfaction

One of the most critical factors in delivering exceptional IT services is ensuring customer satisfaction. It not only helps in maintaining strong relationships with customers but also contributes to the overall success of the business. As an IT manager, it is your responsibility to monitor and measure customer satisfaction regularly. There are various ways to do this, such as conducting surveys, gathering feedback from customer meetings, and analyzing support tickets. The key is to have an open and transparent communication channel with your customers and actively address any concerns or issues they may have. Regularly assessing customer satisfaction will help in identifying areas for improvement and maintaining high levels of service quality. In addition to traditional methods, utilizing technology solutions such as customer satisfaction tracking software can also aid in monitoring satisfaction levels. These tools provide real-time data, allowing you to address any issues or concerns promptly. They also provide insights into customer behaviors and preferences, which can help in improving service levels.

Overall, monitoring customer satisfaction is crucial for ensuring that your team is meeting SLAs and providing excellent IT services. It also provides an opportunity for you to showcase the value of IT services to the business and build strong relationships with your customers.

Closing Thoughts

In conclusion, as an IT manager, setting and measuring service levels and monitoring customer satisfaction are integral parts of your role. By setting clear and realistic SLAs, continuously measuring and improving service levels, and monitoring customer satisfaction, you can ensure that your team delivers exceptional and value-added services to the business. Remember to involve your team throughout the process and encourage a culture of continuous improvement to achieve the highest levels of service quality.

Chapter 16: Performance Management for IT Teams

Today's successful IT managers must not only possess a deep understanding of technology, but also strong people management skills. Central to effective people management is the process of performance management, which includes performance evaluations, goal setting and expectations, and performance improvement plans. In this chapter, we will discuss how IT managers can use performance management techniques to help their teams thrive and achieve their fullest potential.

Performance Evaluations

Performance evaluations, also known as performance appraisals or reviews, are an essential part of performance management. They provide a structured way for managers to assess their team members' performance, identify areas for improvement, and recognize achievements. When conducting performance evaluations, it is important for IT managers to use a fair and objective approach. This means basing evaluations on measurable criteria, such as project outcomes, team contributions, and individual goals. It is also crucial to provide constructive feedback, both positive and negative, and to give team members a chance to respond and ask questions. Additionally, performance evaluations should be an ongoing process rather than a once-a-year event. Regular check-ins and feedback sessions can help managers and team members stay on track and make necessary adjustments throughout the year.

Setting Goals and Expectations

One of the most important aspects of performance management is setting clear goals and expectations for team members. This not only gives employees a sense of direction and purpose, but also helps them understand how their individual contributions contribute to the overall success of the team and the organization. When setting goals and expectations, it is important for IT managers to align them with the company's overall objectives and the employee's role and skill set. Goals should also be specific, measurable, achievable, relevant, and time-bound (SMART) to ensure they are attainable and meaningful.

In addition to setting goals, managers must also communicate their expectations clearly and consistently. This not only helps employees understand what is expected of them, but also reduces confusion and conflict.

Performance Improvement Plans

Despite the best efforts of managers and team members, there may be times when performance falls below expectations. In such cases, it is important for IT managers to implement performance improvement plans (PIPs) to help team members get back on track. A PIP is a structured plan that outlines specific steps for improvement and sets a timeline for achieving them. It is important for managers to involve the team members in the development of the PIP and provide them with the support and resources they need to succeed.

While PIPs are often viewed as a last resort before disciplinary action, they can also be used proactively to help team members reach their full potential. By identifying areas for improvement and providing a structured plan for growth, PIPs can help drive performance and elevate team members to new levels of success.

In Summary

Performance management is a vital part of an IT manager's role. By conducting fair and objective performance evaluations, setting clear goals and expectations, and implementing performance improvement plans when necessary, managers can help their teams perform at their best and contribute to the overall success of the organization.

Remember, performance management is an ongoing process that requires regular communication, feedback, and support. By investing time and effort into performance management, IT managers can create a culture of growth and development that will benefit both their team and the organization as a whole.

Chapter 17: Managing IT Risks with Strategic Risk Management

Identifying and Assessing Risks

As an IT manager, you are responsible for the successful execution of projects, maintenance of systems, implementation of new technologies, and overall management of your team. With all of these responsibilities, it is essential to recognize that risk is an inherent part of your job. Risks can manifest in various forms, including financial, legal, technical, and operational. It is crucial to understand these risks and their potential impact on your organization. The first step in managing risk is to identify and assess potential risks. This process involves an ongoing evaluation of your IT infrastructure and operations. It requires you to have a thorough understanding of your organization's goals, objectives, and processes. You must also be aware of any external factors that may impact your operations, such as changing industry regulations or advancements in technology. To identify risks, you can conduct risk assessments that involve analyzing your IT systems, processes, policies, and procedures. This assessment may also involve reviewing historical data, interviewing key stakeholders, and conducting a risk analysis. These assessments can help you determine the likelihood and impact of potential risks on your organization.

Developing Risk Management Strategies

Once potential risks have been identified and assessed, the next step is to develop risk management strategies. These strategies involve developing plans and procedures to mitigate, monitor, and control risks. The goal is to reduce the likelihood of risks occurring and minimize their impact if they do. When developing risk management strategies, it is essential to involve key stakeholders, including your team, senior management, and external experts. It is also essential to consider the potential financial and operational impact of these strategies and weigh them against the potential risk.

Some common risk management strategies include risk avoidance, risk transfer, risk reduction, and risk acceptance. Risk avoidance involves avoiding the risk altogether by not engaging in activities that may lead to it. Risk transfer involves transferring the risk to a third party, such as an insurance company. Risk reduction involves taking measures to minimize the likelihood or impact of the risk. Lastly, risk acceptance involves acknowledging the risk and having a plan in place to mitigate its impact.

Contingency Planning

Despite your best efforts, risks may still occur. In these situations, having a well-developed contingency plan is essential. A contingency plan is a set of measures put in place to handle unexpected events and minimize their impact on your organization. Contingency plans should be created for each potential risk identified during the risk assessment. They should outline specific steps to take in case the risk materializes. These plans should also include a timeline for implementation and identify who is responsible for executing each step. It is crucial to review and update contingency plans regularly as new risks may arise, and existing risks may change in likelihood or impact. By having well-developed contingency plans in place, your organization can handle any risk that may occur with minimal disruption to operations.

In Conclusion

Risk management is a vital part of being an IT manager. By identifying and assessing potential risks, developing effective risk management strategies, and having contingency plans in place, you can mitigate risks and minimize their impact on your organization. Remember to involve key stakeholders, regularly review and update your risk management strategies, and always be prepared with contingency plans. By effectively managing risks, you can ensure the success of your projects, the stability of your operations, and the overall success of your organization.

Chapter 18: Managing IT Projects Portfolio

In today's fast-paced business environment, technology is constantly evolving and organizations are constantly seeking ways to stay ahead of the game. As a result, project management has become a crucial aspect of IT management. IT projects are the driving force behind an organization's growth and success, and it is the responsibility of an IT manager to oversee and manage these projects effectively.

Prioritizing Projects

One of the biggest challenges IT managers face is deciding which projects to prioritize. With limited resources, it is essential to carefully select and prioritize projects to ensure the most impactful and valuable ones are given the necessary attention and resources. The first step in prioritizing projects is to align them with the company's overall business goals. This means understanding the organization's strategic objectives and determining which projects will contribute the most towards achieving those goals. IT managers should also consider the potential risks and benefits associated with each project and how they align with the company's risk appetite and growth plans.

Another useful framework for prioritizing projects is the MoSCoW method. This approach categorizes projects as Must-Have, Should-Have, Could-Have, and Won't-Have. This helps IT managers focus on the most critical projects and determine which ones can be deferred or eliminated.

Portfolio Management Tools and Techniques

Managing an organization's IT projects portfolio requires the use of various tools and techniques. One of the most commonly used tools is a project portfolio management (PPM) system. PPM software allows IT managers to track and prioritize projects, allocate resources, and monitor progress. It also provides a clear overview of the entire project portfolio and enables decision-making based on data and analytics rather than guesswork. Another important tool is a project management methodology, such as Agile or Waterfall. These methodologies provide a structured approach to planning, executing, and monitoring projects. They also help IT managers mitigate risks and address any issues that arise during the project lifecycle.

In addition to tools, IT managers can also use various techniques to effectively manage their project portfolio. For example, using techniques such as cost-benefit analysis and Net Present Value (NPV) helps identify which projects will have the greatest impact on the organization's bottom line. Similarly, the use of resource management techniques, such as resource leveling and resource smoothing, ensures optimal resource allocation across the project portfolio.

Aligning Projects with Business Goals

As mentioned earlier, it is crucial to align IT projects with the organization's business goals. This alignment ensures that the projects being undertaken will have a significant impact on the overall success of the company. It also helps IT managers justify project budgets and gain support from senior management. To align projects with business goals, IT managers should communicate with key stakeholders and understand their expectations. Regular status updates and progress reports should also be shared with stakeholders to keep them informed and engaged in the project. Additionally, IT managers should establish and regularly review Key Performance Indicators (KPIs) for each project to ensure that they are on track to meet business goals. It is also essential to regularly reassess the project portfolio to ensure that the projects being undertaken are still aligned with the company's current business objectives. This review process should be done at least once a year to make necessary adjustments and realign projects with the organization's evolving goals.

In Conclusion

Managing an IT projects portfolio is a complex and dynamic task. With limited resources and changing business goals, IT managers must carefully prioritize, monitor, and adjust projects to ensure successful outcomes. By using appropriate tools, techniques, and alignment with business goals, IT managers can effectively manage their project portfolio and drive their organization towards success.

Chapter 19: Aligning IT Strategy with Business Strategy

Aligning IT Strategy with Business Strategy

As an IT Manager, one of your primary responsibilities is to ensure that the IT strategy aligns with the overall business strategy. In today's digital age, technology plays a critical role in driving business success and competitiveness. It is essential to have a clear understanding of the business goals and objectives to develop and execute an effective IT strategy that supports them. A fundamental aspect of aligning IT strategy with business strategy is to establish a strong partnership between the IT department and other departments within the organization. This collaboration and communication are crucial in understanding the business needs and how technology can help achieve those goals.

To succeed in aligning IT strategy with business strategy, it is essential to have a thorough understanding of the company's products, services, and operations. This knowledge will help you identify opportunities where technology can be leveraged to improve processes, reduce costs, and add value to the organization.

Forecasting Future Technology Needs

Technology is evolving at an unprecedented pace, and as an IT Manager, it is your responsibility to stay ahead of the curve and anticipate future technology needs. By forecasting future technology needs, you can ensure that the IT strategy is sustainable and adaptable to meet the organization's changing needs. One key tool for forecasting future technology needs is conducting regular technology assessments. This involves evaluating the current technology landscape, identifying potential areas for improvement, and considering emerging technologies that could benefit the organization in the future.

Additionally, staying informed about industry trends and innovations is essential in forecasting future technology needs. Attend conferences, read industry publications, and network with other IT professionals to gain insights into emerging technologies and how they can impact your organization.

Strategic Planning Tools

To align IT strategy with business strategy, you need to have a strategic planning framework in place. There are several strategic planning tools that can assist you in this process. Some of the most effective tools include SWOT analysis, PESTLE analysis, and Porter's Five Forces. SWOT analysis helps identify an organization's strengths, weaknesses, opportunities, and threats, providing valuable insights into where technology can play a significant role. PESTLE analysis considers external factors such as political, economic, legal, and environmental factors that can impact an organization's operations and assist in developing a strategic plan that takes these factors into account. Porter's Five Forces analysis is a tool that helps evaluate the level of competition within an industry and identifies areas where technology can help gain a competitive advantage.

Other strategic planning tools that can be useful in aligning IT strategy with business strategy include Balanced Scorecard, Growth-Share Matrix, and Value Chain Analysis. It is essential to select the appropriate tool(s) that best align with your organization's unique needs and objectives.

In Conclusion

As an IT Manager, it is crucial to align IT strategy with business strategy to ensure the organization's success. This alignment requires a strong partnership with other departments, a thorough understanding of the company's operations, and the use of strategic planning tools to forecast future technology needs. By leveraging these strategies, you can position your organization for success in the dynamic and ever-changing technology landscape.

Chapter 20: IT Manager's Handbook - Mastering IT Training

Identifying Training Needs

As an IT manager, one of your main responsibilities is to ensure that your team has the necessary skills and knowledge to effectively carry out their duties. This means constantly identifying any gaps in their skills and providing training opportunities to fill those gaps. Identifying training needs can be a daunting task, but it is a crucial step in developing a high-performing IT team. The first step in identifying training needs is to assess the current skills and knowledge of your team. This can be done through performance evaluations, team meetings, or one-on-one conversations. Take note of any areas where your team may be lacking or struggling. You can also gather feedback from your team on what skills they feel they need to improve on.

Another important factor to consider when identifying training needs is the current and future goals of your organization. Are there any upcoming projects or initiatives that will require new skills or knowledge from your team? Are there any new technologies or processes that your team will need to learn in order to stay competitive? Keeping these factors in mind can help you identify specific training needs for your team.

Creating Training Programs

Once you have identified the training needs of your team, the next step is to create a training program that meets those needs. This requires careful planning and consideration to ensure that the training program is effective and engaging for your team. Start by determining the objectives of the training program. What specific skills or knowledge do you want your team to gain from the training? This will help you select the appropriate training methods and materials. There are various training methods available, such as classroom training, online courses, workshops, and on-the-job training. Consider the learning styles of your team and choose the methods that will be most effective for them. It is also important to source training materials from reputable sources and to ensure they are up-to-date and relevant to your team's needs. Another important factor to consider when creating a training program is the time and resources available. It is important to set realistic timelines and allocate resources accordingly to ensure the success of the training program. You may also want to involve your team in the planning process to gather their input and make them feel more invested in the training.

Measuring Training Effectiveness

After implementing a training program, it is essential to measure its effectiveness to determine if it was worth the time and resources invested. This involves setting metrics and gathering feedback from your team. One way to measure the effectiveness of a training program is to track the progress and improvement of your team members. Keep tabs on their performance and performance indicators before and after the training to see if there is a noticeable improvement. You can also gather feedback from your team through surveys or one-on-one conversations to see how they perceived the training and if they found it helpful. It is also important to consider the impact of the training on the overall performance of your team and the organization. Did the training result in a more efficient and productive team? Did it help achieve the organization's goals? These factors can also be used to measure the effectiveness of a training program.

In conclusion, identifying training needs, creating effective training programs, and measuring their effectiveness are crucial steps in developing a high-performing IT team. With the rapidly changing landscape of technology, continuous learning is essential for IT professionals to stay competitive. As an IT manager, it is your responsibility to provide your team with the necessary training to keep them updated and to help them reach their full potential. By following these steps, you can ensure that your team is well-equipped to face any challenge and contribute to the success of your organization.

Chapter 21: The Art of IT Compliance

Understanding IT Compliance

As technology continues to advance at a rapid pace, businesses are facing increasingly complex regulatory requirements. This means that IT managers must not only keep up with the latest advancements in technology, but also must ensure that their organization remains compliant with various regulations. But what exactly is IT compliance and why is it important? IT compliance refers to adhering to laws, regulations, and standards that relate to technology operations and data management. These regulations vary depending on the industry and type of organization, but can include things such as data security, data privacy, and recordkeeping requirements. Failure to comply with these regulations can result in hefty fines, legal consequences, and damage to the organization's reputation.

Implementing Controls

To stay compliant with regulations, IT managers must implement adequate controls within their organization's IT systems and processes. This involves conducting risk assessments to identify areas of vulnerability and developing strategies to mitigate those risks. Common controls include encryption, firewalls, access controls, and data backup protocols.

But it's not enough to simply have these controls in place. IT managers must also regularly monitor and test these controls to ensure they are functioning effectively and making adjustments as needed. This requires a strong understanding of the organization's infrastructure and potential vulnerabilities.

Staying Compliant with Regulations

Staying compliant with regulations can seem like a daunting task for IT managers, especially as regulations continue to evolve and become more complex. However, there are a few key strategies that can help IT managers stay on top of compliance requirements and avoid any legal or financial consequences. One important strategy is to stay informed about current and upcoming regulations. This can be done through attending industry conferences, networking with other IT professionals, and regularly monitoring industry publications and updates from regulatory bodies. Another crucial aspect is maintaining detailed documentation of all IT processes and activities. This documentation can serve as evidence of compliance in the event of an audit or investigation. Regular audits of IT systems and processes can also help identify any non-compliant practices and allow for corrective action before it becomes a larger issue. Additionally, building a culture of compliance within the organization is essential. This means involving employees at all levels in understanding and adhering to regulations. Training programs, clear policies and procedures, and regular communication can help achieve this culture of compliance.

Conclusion

Ensuring IT compliance is a critical responsibility for IT managers, and it requires a deep understanding of regulations, risk management, and effective controls and practices. By continually staying informed and implementing a culture of compliance within the organization, IT managers can successfully navigate the complex regulatory landscape and protect their organization from potential consequences.

Chapter 22: Building and Managing Virtual Teams

The world of business is constantly evolving, and with the rise of technology, the concept of a physical workplace is becoming more and more obsolete. This is especially true for the field of information technology, where virtual teams have become the norm rather than the exception. As an IT manager, you may find yourself faced with the challenge of managing a team that is spread across various locations, time zones, and even cultures. It may seem like a daunting task, but fear not - with effective communication, overcoming challenges, and building a cohesive team, you can successfully manage a virtual team and achieve great success.

Effective Communication

Communication is the key to the success of any team, but it becomes even more crucial when managing a virtual team. Without the luxury of face-to-face interactions, it is essential to establish effective means of communication to keep your team connected and on the same page. This means utilizing various communication tools such as email, video conferencing, instant messaging, and project management platforms. It is important to establish guidelines and expectations for communication, including response times and preferred methods of communication. Regularly scheduled check-ins and team meetings can also help ensure that everyone is working towards the same goals and staying updated on project progress.

In addition to utilizing technology for communication, it is also essential to foster a culture of open and transparent communication within the team. This means encouraging team members to share their thoughts, concerns, and ideas openly and respectfully. As the manager, you should also be proactive in seeking feedback and addressing any issues that may arise. By cultivating a culture of effective communication, you can build trust and strengthen the relationships within your virtual team.

Overcoming Challenges

Managing a virtual team comes with its own unique set of challenges. One of the main challenges is establishing trust and team cohesion amongst team members who may have never met in person. This can be overcome by creating opportunities for team members to get to know each other on a personal level. This could include virtual team building activities, icebreaker questions during meetings, and even setting aside time for casual conversation before diving into work discussions. Another challenge is ensuring that all team members are on the same page and working towards the same goals. This can be addressed by setting clear expectations and guidelines for project work, deadlines, and communication. It is also important to regularly check-in with team members and provide them with the necessary support and resources to ensure that they can successfully complete their tasks.

Building a Cohesive Team

A successful virtual team is one that works together seamlessly, despite not being physically together. To achieve this, it is crucial to foster a sense of teamwork and collaboration. This can be done by encouraging open communication, recognizing and celebrating individual and team successes, and providing opportunities for team members to work together on projects. Collaboration tools such as shared documents and virtual whiteboards can also help promote teamwork and facilitate the sharing of ideas and feedback.

In addition to promoting teamwork, it is also important to create a positive work environment within the virtual team. This means fostering a culture of respect, appreciation, and inclusivity. As the manager, it is your responsibility to lead by example and ensure that all team members feel valued and supported. By building a cohesive team, you can increase productivity and create a positive work culture, even within a virtual setting.

In Conclusion

Managing a virtual team may come with its own set of challenges, but with effective communication, overcoming obstacles, and building a cohesive team, you can successfully navigate these challenges and create a high-performing virtual team. As an IT manager, it is crucial to adapt to the changing landscape of the workplace, and with the right strategies and mindset, you can lead your virtual team to success. By fostering a culture of open communication, trust, and teamwork, you can achieve great things with your virtual team. Remember to embrace technology, be proactive in addressing challenges, and always prioritize fostering a positive work environment for your team.

Chapter 23: Leveraging Cloud Computing for IT Management

Understanding Benefits and Risks

Cloud computing has revolutionized the way businesses operate, and IT managers must stay on top of this constantly evolving technology to remain competitive in today's fast-paced business world. By harnessing the power of cloud computing, IT managers can streamline processes, improve efficiency, and reduce costs. However, like any new technology, there are also risks associated with moving to the cloud. As an IT manager, it is crucial to understand both the benefits and the risks of implementing cloud solutions.

Implementing Cloud Solutions

When it comes to implementing cloud solutions, it is essential to have a clear understanding of your organization's needs and goals. With the numerous options available, it can be challenging to determine which cloud services will best meet your specific requirements. As an IT manager, it is your responsibility to evaluate your organization's needs and choose the right cloud service provider. This decision involves considering factors such as data security, reliability, scalability, and cost. With cloud computing, IT managers can say goodbye to the days of physical servers taking up valuable office space. The cloud offers scalable, on-demand resources that can be easily accessed from anywhere with an internet connection. By moving to the cloud, IT managers can eliminate the need to invest in expensive hardware and equipment. This shift can significantly reduce costs and increase efficiency, allowing IT managers to focus on more critical tasks such as strategy and innovation. In addition to the cost and efficiency benefits, the cloud also offers greater flexibility and agility. With the ability to access resources on-demand, IT managers can quickly scale up or down their IT infrastructure as needed. This adaptability is especially useful during peak periods or when unexpected demands arise. However, like any technology, there are risks associated with moving to the cloud. One of the biggest concerns for IT managers is data security. When data is stored in the cloud, it is essential to ensure that proper security measures are in place to protect sensitive information. IT managers must work closely with cloud service providers to ensure that proper security protocols are in place, such as encryption and access controls. Another risk to consider is the potential for service interruptions or outages. While cloud service providers typically offer high levels of reliability and uptime, these issues can still occur. IT managers must have contingency plans in place to handle any disruptions in service to minimize the impact on business operations.

Managing Cloud Vendors

The success of implementing cloud solutions depends heavily on the relationship between an IT manager and their cloud service provider. As the liaison between the organization and the cloud vendor, IT managers must effectively manage this partnership to ensure that the organization's needs are being met consistently. Communication is key in maintaining a healthy relationship with a cloud service provider. IT managers should regularly communicate with the vendor to ensure that any issues are quickly addressed and resolved. This open communication can also help in negotiating contracts and contract renewals. Managing vendor contracts is another crucial responsibility of an IT manager when it comes to cloud solutions. IT managers must ensure that contracts are well-defined, outlining service levels, costs, and security protocols. As the organization's needs evolve, IT managers must also review and update contracts to ensure they align with current requirements. Another crucial aspect of managing cloud vendors is monitoring performance. IT managers must regularly review their cloud service provider's performance against agreed-upon service levels to ensure that the organization is receiving the level of service they expect. If performance falls short, IT managers must address the issue with the vendor and work towards a resolution.

In conclusion, cloud computing is an integral part of the modern IT environment. With its numerous benefits, such as cost efficiency, flexibility, and scalability, it has become a vital tool for IT managers. However, along with these benefits come potential risks that IT managers must carefully assess and manage. By understanding the benefits and risks of implementing cloud solutions and effectively managing relationships with cloud vendors, IT managers can successfully leverage cloud computing to drive business success.

Chapter 24: IT Governance and Leadership

Establishing a Governance Framework

In today's fast-paced and technology-driven world, it is crucial for businesses to have an effective and well-structured IT governance framework. This framework provides a structure for decision-making processes, risk management, and compliance. As an IT manager, it is your responsibility to establish a governance framework that aligns with your organization's objectives and supports the overall business strategy. A strong and well-defined governance framework can help your IT department to function efficiently and effectively, ensuring the success of your organization. One of the key components of an IT governance framework is defining roles and responsibilities. This involves clearly outlining the responsibilities of different teams and individuals within the IT department, as well as clarifying the communication and reporting channels. This helps avoid confusion and overlaps in roles and ensures that everyone knows their responsibilities and who to report to. It also ensures that decision-making processes are transparent and well-documented.

Another important aspect of a governance framework is establishing policies and procedures. These are the guidelines and rules that govern how IT operations are conducted within the organization. They cover areas such as security, procurement, project management, and risk management. These policies and procedures should be clearly defined, communicated, and regularly reviewed and updated to ensure they are aligned with the ever-changing IT landscape and business needs.

Decision-Making Processes

Effective decision-making processes are essential for the success of any IT department. With the rapid pace of technological advancements, IT managers are faced with multiple decisions every day, and it is crucial to have a structured approach to make informed and effective decisions. This is where an IT governance framework comes into play. It provides a structure for decision-making processes, ensuring that they are aligned with the overall business objectives and that the decisions are documented and communicated appropriately. An important aspect of decision-making processes is involving stakeholders. These may include senior management, end-users, and other departments within the organization. By involving stakeholders, you can gather different perspectives and ideas, which can help make more informed decisions. It also ensures that the decisions made are aligned with the needs and priorities of the entire organization.

Effective communication is also crucial in decision-making processes. It is important to keep all stakeholders informed and involved throughout the decision-making process. This can prevent miscommunication and ensure that everyone is on the same page. It is also important to communicate the rationale behind the decisions made, as this promotes transparency and helps stakeholders understand the thought process behind the decision.

Effective Leadership Techniques

As an IT manager, your leadership skills play a crucial role in the success of your IT department and the organization as a whole. Effective leadership involves not only managing tasks and operations but also managing people. It is important to provide a positive and motivating work environment for your team, where they feel supported and valued. One important aspect of effective leadership is setting a clear vision and goals for the IT department. This provides direction and purpose for your team and helps them understand their role in the larger picture. It is also important to lead by example and exhibit the qualities you want to see in your team, such as adaptability, open-mindedness, and problem-solving skills. Another crucial aspect of effective leadership is communication. As an IT manager, you need to be a strong communicator, both verbally and in writing. You need to be able to clearly articulate the vision and goals of the IT department, as well as explain complex technical concepts to non-technical stakeholders. Good communication also involves active listening and being open to feedback and ideas from your team. In today's rapidly evolving business landscape, it is important for IT managers to be adaptable and open to change. This involves being able to embrace new technologies and ways of working, as well as being open-minded to new ideas and perspectives. A successful IT manager should also be able to effectively manage and navigate through change, ensuring that the IT department is always aligned with the organization's goals and objectives.

In conclusion, establishing a governance framework, effective decision-making processes, and utilizing strong leadership techniques are crucial for IT managers to navigate the complex and ever-changing IT landscape successfully. By aligning your IT department with the overall business strategy and involving stakeholders in decision-making processes, you can ensure the success of your organization. Effective leadership skills also play a crucial role in creating a positive work environment and driving your team towards success. As an IT manager, it is your responsibility to constantly review and improve your governance framework and leadership techniques to stay ahead of the curve and drive your organization towards success.

Chapter 25: IT Project Management Office (PMO)

Functions of a PMO

The IT Project Management Office (PMO) is a centralized team responsible for defining and maintaining the project management standards and processes within an organization. The main function of a PMO is to act as a central hub for project management activities, providing guidance, support, and oversight to ensure projects are delivered on time, within budget, and with expected results. PMOs play a crucial role in streamlining project-related activities and driving consistent project management practices across the organization. One of the key functions of a PMO is to establish and maintain project management best practices. This includes developing and implementing standard methodologies, templates, and tools to be used by all project managers within the organization. By establishing a standardized approach, the PMO enables seamless collaboration and communication among project teams, ensuring that all projects are executed in a consistent and efficient manner.

Another important function of a PMO is to provide support and guidance to project managers. This may include offering training programs, coaching sessions, and mentoring to enhance the project management skills of the team. The PMO may also assist in resource allocation, budget management, and risk mitigation to ensure projects stay on track and on budget.

Setting up a PMO

Setting up a PMO is a complex and multi-step process that requires careful planning and execution. The first step in establishing a PMO is to determine the purpose and scope of the PMO. This includes defining the functions, responsibilities, and services the PMO will provide to the organization. Once the purpose and scope are defined, the PMO team can then identify the stakeholders and obtain buy-in from key decision-makers within the organization. The next step is to develop a PMO charter, which outlines the goals, objectives, and expectations of the PMO. This charter will serve as a roadmap for the PMO team and provide a clear direction for the PMO's activities. After the charter is developed, the PMO team can then start to establish the project management methodology, processes, and tools that will be used by project teams. This includes defining project life cycle phases, project governance structure, project management templates, and other project management artifacts. It is essential for the PMO team to keep the project management processes simple and easy to follow, as overly complicated processes can hinder project execution and add unnecessary burden to project teams. Once the project management processes and tools are established, the PMO can then focus on building the PMO team. Hiring or assigning the right personnel with relevant project management experience is crucial in ensuring the success of a PMO. The PMO team members should possess a blend of technical expertise, project management skills, and interpersonal skills to effectively lead and support project teams.

Finally, the PMO team must promote the PMO and its services across the organization. This may include conducting training sessions, hosting informational workshops, or developing marketing materials to create awareness and generate interest in the PMO.

Measuring PMO Success

Measuring the success of a PMO is crucial in determining its effectiveness and showcasing its value to the organization. There are various metrics and methods that can be used to measure PMO success, including:

Project Success Rates:

One way to measure the success of a PMO is by tracking project success rates. This includes measuring the percentage of projects delivered within the set timeframe, budget, and expected outcomes. By consistently delivering successful projects, the PMO demonstrates its ability to drive successful project outcomes and add value to the organization.

Budget and Time Savings:

The PMO can also be measured by the amount of cost and time savings achieved through project management standardization and process improvements. By establishing efficient project management processes, the PMO can help reduce project costs and delivery time while maintaining quality and meeting project objectives.

Stakeholder Satisfaction:

Another important measure of PMO success is stakeholder satisfaction. This includes obtaining feedback from project managers, team members, and other stakeholders on the effectiveness and value of the PMO's services. By regularly soliciting feedback and addressing any concerns or suggestions, the PMO can continuously improve its processes and ensure stakeholder satisfaction.

Process Adherence and Compliance:

A well-functioning PMO should have processes and standards that are adhered to by all project teams. By measuring process adherence and compliance, the PMO can ensure that project teams are following the established standards and identify any areas for improvement. In addition to these metrics, the PMO can also conduct periodic assessments, project audits, and benchmarking to measure its success and identify areas for improvement.

In conclusion, a well-structured and efficient PMO is instrumental in driving successful project outcomes and helping organizations achieve their strategic objectives. By understanding the functions of a PMO, following a strategic approach in setting up a PMO, and regularly measuring its success, organizations can establish a strong PMO that adds value and promotes project success.

Chapter 26: Managing the IT Budget

Managing an IT budget requires skill, strategy, and foresight. As an IT manager, it is your responsibility to create and manage a budget that aligns with your company's goals and objectives. In this chapter, we will discuss the essential elements of creating a budget plan, forecasting and tracking expenses, and making budget revisions and adjustments. Let's dive into the world of budget management and learn how to master it with confidence.

Creating a Budget Plan

A budget plan is a roadmap that outlines your company's financial goals and objectives for a specific period, usually a fiscal year. As an IT manager, you must work closely with your team to plan and create a budget that supports the company's overall strategy. The first step in creating a budget plan is to identify your company's priorities and align them with your IT department's goals. It is crucial to involve all stakeholders and decision-makers in this process to ensure that their needs and expectations are reflected in the budget.

Once you have a clear understanding of your company's priorities and goals, you can start estimating the expenses associated with each IT project or initiative. Take into consideration the cost of hardware, software, infrastructure, personnel, training, and any other expenses that may arise. It is essential to be as accurate as possible in estimating expenses to avoid any surprises down the road.

Forecasting and Tracking Expenses

Forecasting and tracking expenses are vital parts of budget management. By forecasting potential expenses, you can anticipate and prepare for any potential budgetary constraints. It also allows you to make informed decisions when it comes to allocating funds to different projects and initiatives. As an IT manager, you must work closely with your team to ensure that they are tracking their expenses and reporting them accurately and in a timely manner.

There are various tools and methods you can use to track expenses, such as spreadsheets, budgeting software, and regular budget meetings with your team. Whichever method you choose, make sure it is transparent and accessible to all stakeholders. By keeping a close eye on expenses, you can identify any discrepancies and take necessary measures to address them promptly.

Budget Revisions and Adjustments

Despite the best planning and forecasting, unexpected expenses can arise, and your budget may need to be revised and adjusted. It is crucial to have a contingency plan in place for such situations and be prepared to make necessary changes to keep the budget on track. As an IT manager, you must be flexible and adaptable to adjust the budget as needed while keeping the company's goals and objectives in mind. Before making any budget revisions or adjustments, it is essential to review the changes with all stakeholders and get their approval. Transparency and communication are key factors in successfully managing a budget. By involving all decision-makers and stakeholders in the process, you can ensure that everyone is on the same page and working towards the same goal.

In Conclusion

Managing an IT budget is a crucial aspect of being an IT manager. By creating a budget plan, forecasting and tracking expenses, and making necessary revisions and adjustments, you can ensure that your IT department is aligned with the company's goals and objectives. Remember to involve all stakeholders and decision-makers in the budgeting process and communicate any changes or updates effectively. With a well-managed budget, you can confidently lead your team towards success.

Chapter 27: Business Continuity and Disaster Recovery Management

Developing a Business Continuity Plan

As an IT manager, it is crucial to have a well-defined and comprehensive business continuity plan (BCP) in place to ensure the smooth functioning of your organization in the event of a disaster. A BCP is a proactive approach to dealing with potential risks and disruptions that could interrupt business operations and impact the IT infrastructure. It helps to minimize the effects of the disaster and enables companies to quickly resume their normal operations. To develop an effective BCP, it is essential to conduct a thorough risk assessment to identify potential threats and vulnerabilities. This includes natural disasters such as floods, hurricanes, and earthquakes, as well as man-made disasters like cyber attacks, power outages, and human error. Prioritizing these risks will help to allocate resources more efficiently and focus on critical areas of the business. Once the risks have been identified, the next step is to create an actionable plan. This plan should include detailed procedures and protocols for responding to different types of disasters. It should also identify key personnel and their roles and responsibilities during a crisis. A communication plan should also be developed to ensure seamless communication between all stakeholders during a disaster.

Disaster Recovery Testing

Having a well-defined BCP is not enough; it is equally important to regularly test and update it to ensure its effectiveness. Disaster recovery testing is the process of simulating a disaster to evaluate the BCP's response and identify any gaps or weaknesses. There are various types of disaster recovery tests, including walk-through exercises, structured walkthroughs, and full-scale drills. Walk-through exercises involve discussing and reviewing the plan with key stakeholders to identify any inconsistencies or gaps. Structured walkthroughs involve conducting a step-by-step review of the plan, and full-scale drills are a simulation of an actual disaster scenario to test the plan's response in real-time.

Regular testing helps to identify potential issues and make necessary adjustments to the plan. It also allows key personnel to become familiar with their roles and responsibilities and identify any training gaps that need to be addressed.

Responding to Disasters

Disasters can strike at any time, and it is crucial to have a well-coordinated response plan in place to minimize the impact on business operations. The BCP should specify the steps to be taken in the event of a disaster, including activating emergency procedures, initiating the communication plan, and restoring critical systems. In the event of a disaster, the first priority is to ensure the safety of employees. Once this is taken care of, the focus shifts to assessing the damage and implementing recovery procedures. This may involve shifting operations to alternate sites, restoring backups, and replacing damaged hardware. The IT manager's role is critical in coordinating the response effort, communicating with stakeholders, and ensuring the timely restoration of IT services. In addition to responding to the immediate crisis, it is crucial to have a plan for long-term recovery. This may involve evaluating the cause of the disaster and making necessary changes to prevent future occurrences. It may also include implementing lessons learned from the disaster to improve the BCP and strengthen the organization's resilience.

Conclusion

In today's fast-paced business environment, disasters can happen at any time, and the impact on IT infrastructure can be catastrophic. As an IT manager, it is your responsibility to ensure the organization is prepared to handle such events and minimize their impact on the business. Developing a business continuity plan, regularly testing it, and having a well-coordinated response to disasters are crucial components of effective disaster recovery management. By following these best practices, you can ensure the smooth functioning of your organization, even in the face of adversity.

Chapter 28: Stakeholder Management: Building Strong Relationships

As an IT manager, one of your key responsibilities is stakeholder management. Stakeholders include anyone who has an interest or influence in your organization's IT projects and initiatives. These can include senior executives, department heads, end-users, vendors, and even customers. Effectively managing these relationships is crucial for the success of your IT projects and for the overall success of your organization.

In this chapter, we will discuss the importance of identifying and prioritizing stakeholders, building strong relationships, and implementing effective stakeholder management strategies.

Identifying and Prioritizing Stakeholders:

The first step in stakeholder management is identifying who your stakeholders are. This involves understanding their level of interest and influence in your IT projects. Some stakeholders may have a direct impact on the project, while others may have a more indirect role. It's crucial to identify all stakeholders, no matter how small their role may seem. Once you have identified your stakeholders, it's important to prioritize them. This can be done by categorizing them into groups based on their level of interest and influence. For example, high-interest stakeholders with a high level of influence should receive more attention and communication compared to low-interest stakeholders with a low level of influence.

Building Relationships:

Building strong relationships with stakeholders is key to successful stakeholder management. As an IT manager, it's important to establish trust and credibility with your stakeholders. This can be achieved through effective communication, active listening, and demonstrating a genuine interest in their needs and concerns.

Building relationships with stakeholders also involves understanding their expectations. This can be done by regularly engaging with them, conducting surveys, and gathering feedback. By understanding their expectations, you can better align your IT projects and initiatives with their needs and goals.

Stakeholder Management Strategies:

Effective stakeholder management requires a strategic approach. In order to manage multiple stakeholders with different needs and priorities, IT managers must have a clear plan in place. Here are a few strategies to help you manage your stakeholders effectively:

1. Regular Communication: Maintaining open and transparent communication with stakeholders is essential. This includes providing regular updates on project progress, changes, and potential challenges.

2. Establish a Feedback Loop: Encouraging stakeholders to provide feedback and actively listening to their concerns can help build trust and ensure their needs are being met.

3. Set Clear Expectations: Clearly defining the scope, timelines, and goals of your IT projects can help manage stakeholder expectations and avoid potential conflicts.

4. Address Conflict Effectively: Inevitably, there will be conflicts with stakeholders. It's important to address these conflicts promptly and find mutually beneficial solutions.

5. Collaborate and Involve Stakeholders: Involving stakeholders in the decision-making process can help gain their support and commitment to the project. Collaboration also encourages the exchange of ideas and can lead to innovative solutions.

6. Regularly Assess and Adjust: As projects evolve, it's important to continuously assess stakeholder needs and adjust strategies accordingly. Regularly soliciting feedback and conducting assessments can help identify any areas for improvement.

Recap

Managing stakeholders is a critical aspect of an IT manager's role. By identifying and prioritizing stakeholders, building strong relationships, and implementing effective stakeholder management strategies, you can ensure the success of your IT projects and ultimately contribute to the success of your organization. Remember to continuously assess and adjust your stakeholder management approach to best meet their needs and expectations. By following these principles, you can cultivate a positive and collaborative relationship with your stakeholders that will benefit both your IT projects and your organization as a whole.

Chapter 29: Measuring and Improving Performance Using KPIs

Defining KPIs: A Key Element of IT Performance Management

In today's fast-paced and constantly evolving business world, measuring and improving performance is essential for any organization to stay ahead. As an IT manager, it is your responsibility to ensure that your team is performing to the best of their abilities and delivering results that align with the organization's goals. This is where Key Performance Indicators (KPIs) come in. KPIs are specific metrics that organizations use to measure the progress and success of their performance in achieving their goals. These metrics can be quantifiable, such as revenue, or qualitative, such as customer satisfaction. As an IT manager, it is crucial to have a clear understanding of which KPIs are relevant to your team's performance and how to measure them effectively.

The first step in defining KPIs for your team is to identify the organization's overall goals and objectives. This will help you determine which areas to focus on and which KPIs are most relevant. For example, if the organization's goal is to increase customer satisfaction, then a relevant KPI for your IT team can be the percentage of customer issues resolved within an agreed-upon timeframe.

Measuring Performance: The Importance of Accurate Data

Once you have defined the appropriate KPIs, it is essential to have a reliable and accurate data tracking system in place. Data is the backbone of performance measurement and improvement, and without accurate data, it is impossible to assess the team's progress and make informed decisions. One common mistake that IT managers make is relying solely on anecdotal evidence or assumptions when evaluating performance. While these can provide some insights, they do not provide a comprehensive or accurate picture of performance. It is important to have a data-driven approach to performance measurement, ensuring that the metrics used are objective, measurable, and relevant.

To ensure accurate data, it is crucial to have a standardized tracking system in place. This can be as simple as using spreadsheets or as sophisticated as investing in specialized software. Whatever system you choose, make sure it is user-friendly and accessible to all members of your team. Regularly review and validate the data to ensure its accuracy and make adjustments as needed.

Using Metrics to Improve Performance: Setting Targets and Identifying Trends

Aside from providing a means to measure performance, KPIs also serve as a tool for improvement. By consistently tracking and analyzing KPIs, you can identify trends and areas for improvement and set targets for your team to strive towards. The key to improving performance using metrics is to analyze the data in context. Instead of looking at isolated data points, it is important to consider the bigger picture and determine if the current performance is meeting the organization's goals. For example, if your IT team is consistently meeting their target of resolving customer issues within a specific timeframe, but overall customer satisfaction is decreasing, it may be an indication that the KPI needs to be adjusted to better align with the organization's goals. Setting realistic targets based on the data can also motivate and drive your team to achieve better performance. However, it is essential to ensure that the targets are achievable and consider any external factors that may impact performance. Continuously review and adjust targets as needed to ensure they are relevant and challenging yet attainable for your team.

Through the use of KPIs, IT managers can effectively track performance, measure progress, and identify areas for improvement. KPIs provide a data-driven approach to performance management, allowing for more informed decision-making and better alignment with the organization's goals. As an IT manager, it is crucial to have a deep understanding of KPIs and their application to support your team in achieving optimal performance.

Chapter 30: Managing IT Project Risks and Issues

Identifying and Assessing Risks and Issues

As an IT manager, one of your primary responsibilities is to ensure the successful completion of projects within budget and timelines. However, as with any complex undertaking, there are bound to be risks and issues that can potentially derail your project's progress. It is crucial to have a plan in place to identify and assess these risks and issues as early as possible, so you can mitigate their impact on your project's success. To begin with, it is essential to define what constitutes a risk and an issue in the context of IT projects. A risk is any event or circumstance that can have a negative impact on the project's objectives, whereas an issue is a problem that has already arisen and is affecting the project's progress. Risks are potential problems, while issues are actual problems that need to be resolved. To identify risks and issues, you can conduct a risk assessment, which involves analyzing the project's scope, objectives, budget, and timelines to identify any potential threats. This could include factors such as technical challenges, resource constraints, or unforeseen external events. It is also essential to involve your team in this process, as they will have valuable insights into potential risks and issues based on their expertise and experience.

Once you have identified potential risks and issues, the next step is to assess their potential impact on the project. This involves evaluating the likelihood of the risk or issue occurring and its potential severity if it does. You can use tools such as a risk matrix or a probability-impact chart to help with this assessment. It is crucial to assign a level of priority to each risk or issue, so you can focus your efforts on mitigating the most critical risks and addressing the most severe issues.

Implementing Mitigation Strategies

After identifying and assessing risks and issues, the next step is to develop and implement mitigation strategies to minimize their impact on the project. Mitigation strategies can include detailed contingency plans to combat potential risks and immediate action plans to address urgent issues. For risks, you can develop a mitigation plan that outlines steps to prevent the risk from materializing or reducing its impact if it does occur. This plan should include strategies such as conducting additional testing, allocating more resources, or adjusting project timelines. It is also essential to assign responsibility for each risk's mitigation to specific team members, ensuring accountability and follow-through. When it comes to addressing issues, you should have a process in place to identify and report issues as soon as they arise. This could include creating a central issue tracking system, holding regular team meetings to discuss any problems, and encouraging open communication to ensure issues are reported promptly.

A key aspect of implementing mitigation strategies is continuously monitoring and reviewing their effectiveness. As the project progresses, new risks and issues may arise, and existing ones may evolve, so it is essential to regularly review and adjust your mitigation plans accordingly.

Resolving Issues

Despite your best efforts, some issues may still arise during the course of your IT project. It is crucial to have a structured framework in place to resolve these issues effectively and efficiently. The first step is to prioritize the issues based on their potential impact on the project's success. This will allow you to allocate resources accordingly and address the most critical issues first. Next, involve key stakeholders in the resolution process, such as the project sponsor, team members, and external vendors if necessary. This will ensure a collaborative approach to finding solutions and help mitigate any conflicts that may arise. Once a resolution plan is in place, it is essential to communicate the plan and any changes to the project's stakeholders. This will help manage expectations and ensure everyone is on the same page. It is also crucial to have contingency plans in place if the issue persists or escalates, to minimize disruption to the project's progress. After resolving an issue, it is vital to conduct a post-mortem analysis to identify the root cause and assess your team's response to the situation. This will help you identify any process improvements that can be implemented to prevent similar issues in the future.

In Conclusion

As an IT manager, managing risks and issues is an integral part of your job. By following a structured approach to identifying, assessing, and mitigating risks and addressing issues, you can minimize their impact on your project's success. By involving your team and key stakeholders, communicating effectively, and continuously monitoring and reviewing your plans, you can ensure a successful outcome for your IT project.

Chapter 31: Managing IT Partnerships

Managing partnerships is an essential task for IT managers, as they are often responsible for developing and maintaining relationships with external vendors, suppliers, and other businesses. These partnerships can bring great value to an organization, providing access to new technologies, resources, and expertise. However, managing these partnerships requires strategic planning and effective communication to ensure success. In this chapter, we will explore the key steps for managing IT partnerships, from identifying potential partners to measuring their success.

Identifying Potential Partners

The first step in managing IT partnerships is to identify potential partners who can offer value to your organization. This requires a thorough understanding of your organization's needs and goals, as well as the current market trends and available technologies. Consider conducting a SWOT analysis (strengths, weaknesses, opportunities, and threats) to identify any gaps in your IT capabilities and areas where partnering with an external organization could bring significant benefits. It's also essential to conduct thorough research on potential partners. Look for organizations with expertise in areas that align with your organization's needs. Consider their reputation, experience, and track record. It's also vital to evaluate their financial stability and compatibility with your organization's culture and values.

Additionally, networking and attending industry events can be effective ways to identify potential partners and build relationships. This allows you to connect with like-minded individuals and organizations and get a better understanding of their capabilities and values.

Managing Partnerships

Once you have identified potential partners, the next step is to manage the partnerships effectively. This involves creating a partnership agreement that outlines the roles and responsibilities of both parties, including the scope, objectives, and timeline of the partnership. It's essential to have open and honest communication during this process to ensure that both parties are on the same page and have a clear understanding of the expectations. It's also crucial to establish clear communication channels and maintain regular communication with your partners. This ensures that any issues or concerns are addressed promptly and that the partnership stays on track. Regular meetings and status updates can help keep everyone aligned and informed of any changes or updates.

Another aspect of managing partnerships is managing expectations. It's important to set realistic expectations from the beginning and to be transparent about any limitations or challenges that may arise. This allows for a more collaborative and understanding partnership, where both parties work together to overcome obstacles and achieve mutual success.

Measuring Partnership Success

One of the most critical aspects of managing IT partnerships is measuring their success. After all, a partnership that does not bring value to your organization or achieve its intended objectives is not a successful one. It's important to establish key performance indicators (KPIs) and performance metrics to help track the progress of the partnership and its impact on your organization. Some potential KPIs that you can measure include cost savings, improved quality of services, increased efficiency, and improved customer satisfaction. These KPIs will vary depending on the goals and objectives of each partnership. It's essential to determine these KPIs and track them regularly to evaluate the success of the partnership and make any necessary adjustments. Additionally, it's crucial to seek regular feedback from both your internal team and the partner organization. This allows you to get a well-rounded view of the partnership and make any improvements or changes as needed. Evaluating the success of the partnership can also help you determine if it's worth continuing or if it's time to seek out new partnerships that may better align with your current needs and goals.

In conclusion, effective partnership management is essential for IT managers to bring value to their organizations. By identifying potential partners, managing partnerships effectively, and measuring their success, IT managers can ensure that their partnerships are strategic, beneficial, and aligned with the organization's goals. It's crucial to have open and transparent communication, establish clear objectives, and regularly evaluate the partnership's progress. By following these steps, IT managers can build successful and long-lasting partnerships that drive their organization's success.

Chapter 32: Managing Geographically Distributed Teams

Virtual Team Management

In today's globalized world, it is becoming increasingly common for IT teams to work remotely and across different time zones. This brings about a new set of challenges for IT managers, as they are now responsible for managing geographically distributed teams. Virtual team management requires a unique set of skills and strategies to ensure the success and productivity of team members. In this chapter, we will explore the key elements of managing geographically distributed teams and provide valuable insights on how to effectively lead a virtual team.

Overcoming Cultural Differences

One of the main challenges faced by IT managers in managing virtual teams is overcoming cultural differences. With team members located in different parts of the world, diversity in culture, language, and work styles is inevitable. These differences can lead to miscommunication, misunderstandings, and ultimately affect the team's performance. As an IT manager, it is crucial to recognize and address these cultural differences to foster a collaborative and cohesive team dynamic. To overcome cultural differences, IT managers must first educate themselves and their team members on the cultural backgrounds and expectations of each team member. This includes understanding how each culture communicates, their values, work ethic, and preferred communication channels. By being aware of these cultural differences, IT managers can bridge the gap between team members and create a more inclusive work environment.

Another effective way of overcoming cultural differences is by promoting cultural intelligence among team members. Cultural intelligence is the ability to understand and adapt to different cultural contexts. IT managers can encourage this by providing cultural sensitivity training, team-building activities, and encouraging open discussions about cultural differences. By promoting cultural intelligence, virtual teams can function more effectively and minimize any potential conflicts that may arise due to cultural differences.

Effective Communication Strategies

Communication is essential in any team, but it becomes even more critical in virtual teams. When team members are located in different parts of the world, effective communication becomes a key factor in the success of projects. IT managers must ensure that all team members are on the same page when it comes to project expectations, timelines, and deliverables. Here are some communication strategies that IT managers can implement to improve communication within virtual teams:

- Establishing Communication Protocols: IT managers must establish clear communication protocols for team members to follow. This includes setting expectations for response times, preferred communication channels, and guidelines for addressing conflicts or misunderstandings.
- Utilizing Collaboration Tools: In today's digital age, there are numerous collaboration tools available to facilitate communication among virtual teams. From project management software to team messaging platforms, these tools allow team members to communicate in real-time and collaborate on projects.
- Scheduling Regular Meetings: It is crucial for virtual teams to have regular check-ins and meetings to discuss progress, provide updates, and address any concerns. These meetings should be scheduled at a time that is suitable for all team members to ensure maximum participation and engagement.
- Encouraging Open Communication: Virtual teams can sometimes lead to a lack of face-to-face interaction, which can make it challenging for team members to build relationships. IT managers must encourage open communication and create a comfortable environment for team members to share their thoughts and concerns.

In Conclusion

Managing geographically distributed teams requires a unique approach and set of skills from IT managers. By acknowledging cultural differences, promoting cultural intelligence, and implementing effective communication strategies, virtual teams can overcome challenges and thrive in a global work environment. As technology continues to advance and remote work becomes more prevalent, IT managers must equip themselves with the necessary knowledge and skills to effectively manage virtual teams and drive success.

Chapter 33: Managing IT Assets and Configuration Management

Introduction

As an IT manager, one of the most critical areas of responsibility is managing your organization's hardware and software assets. These assets are vital components of your IT infrastructure, and their efficient management can significantly impact your company's bottom line. In this chapter, we will discuss the best practices for managing IT assets and developing effective configuration management strategies. We will also explore some tools that can aid in asset management and configuration management processes.

Managing Hardware and Software Assets

A critical aspect of effective asset management is understanding and keeping track of your organization's hardware and software assets. Hardware assets include any physical devices such as computers, servers, routers, and switches. On the other hand, software assets refer to any applications or programs that run on these devices. The first step in managing IT assets is conducting a comprehensive audit of all hardware and software assets in your organization. This audit should include information on each asset's location, owner, specifications, and license agreements. Once the audit is complete, it is essential to develop a standardized process for tracking and managing assets. This process should include procedures for asset acquisition, deployment, maintenance, and retirement. It should also include protocols for asset disposal to ensure compliance with environmental regulations and data security.

Regular asset audits should be conducted to ensure accurate and up-to-date records. Additionally, creating asset inventory reports can help identify areas for cost savings and optimization. These reports can also assist in tracking IT assets' life cycles, making informed decisions about asset replacements, and predicting future IT hardware and software needs.

Configuration Management Strategies

Configuration management is essential for ensuring consistency and stability in an IT environment. It involves managing changes and updates to hardware and software configurations to maintain a reliable and secure IT infrastructure. Configuration management strategies typically include setting configuration standards, monitoring and tracking changes, and performing regular audits. One of the key components of successful configuration management is creating a centralized repository for tracking asset configurations and changes. This repository should contain information on all asset configurations, including settings, patches, updates, and software versions. This database should also include a record of all configuration changes made, who made them, and when they took place.

Another critical aspect of configuration management is establishing change management processes. Any changes to IT assets should be thoroughly documented and approved before implementation. This process helps prevent any unwanted configurations or unintended consequences.

Tools for Asset Management

Technology can greatly assist in managing IT assets and configurations effectively. Many asset management tools offer features such as automated inventory tracking, centralized repositories, and change management functionalities. These tools can help save time and resources, improve accuracy, and provide real-time data for decision-making. Some popular asset management tools include SolarWinds IT Asset Management, Lansweeper, and Spiceworks. These tools offer a variety of features, including hardware and software inventory management, asset tracking, and reporting capabilities.

In addition to dedicated asset management tools, IT service management (ITSM) platforms can also aid in IT asset management. ITSM tools provide a centralized dashboard for managing IT assets, incidents, and service requests. This integration can streamline IT asset management processes, improve visibility, and increase efficiency.

Conclusion

Efficient asset management and configuration management strategies are essential for a well-functioning IT infrastructure. With a comprehensive understanding of your organization's assets, a standardized process, and the use of appropriate tools, you can effectively manage your IT assets and ensure a stable and secure environment for your company.

Chapter 34: IT Maturity Assessments

Understanding the Importance of Maturity Assessments

The success of any business is dependent on the maturity level of its IT function. An IT maturity assessment helps organizations understand where they stand in terms of their IT capabilities and how they compare to industry standards. It is a valuable tool for measuring the effectiveness and efficiency of IT processes, systems, and strategies.

A maturity assessment provides a comprehensive analysis of an organization's IT strengths, weaknesses, opportunities, and threats. It identifies areas for improvement and outlines a roadmap for achieving the desired level of IT maturity. As an IT manager, conducting regular maturity assessments can help you make informed decisions and prioritize initiatives to drive growth and success for your organization.

Conducting Assessments

There are several methods for conducting an IT maturity assessment, including self-assessment surveys, maturity models, and external assessments performed by consultants. Each method has its benefits and limitations, and the best approach will depend on your organization's goals and resources. Self-assessment surveys are a cost-effective way to gather data and insights from your IT team. It involves distributing questionnaires to IT staff and obtaining input on their perceptions of the organization's IT maturity level. This method can provide a broad view of IT maturity, but may lack objectivity and may not be as comprehensive as other methods. Maturity models, such as the Capability Maturity Model Integration (CMMI) and the Information Technology Infrastructure Library (ITIL), provide a structured framework for assessing IT maturity. Using a maturity model, organizations can benchmark their IT processes against best practices and identify areas for improvement. This method requires more resources and expertise but provides a more detailed and objective assessment.

External assessments involve hiring a consultant to conduct a comprehensive review of your organization's IT maturity level. This usually involves interviews, document reviews, and analysis of IT systems, processes, and strategies. Although more costly, external assessments provide a more in-depth and unbiased evaluation of IT maturity and can offer valuable recommendations for improvement.

Improving IT Maturity

Once an IT maturity assessment is complete, the real work begins. The assessment report will outline areas for improvement and set the foundation for a roadmap for enhancing IT maturity. As an IT manager, your role is critical in driving this transformation and ensuring that your team is equipped to deliver on the organization's objectives. Improving IT maturity requires a holistic approach that involves people, processes, and technology. This may involve investing in training and development for IT staff, implementing standardized processes and procedures, and adopting new technologies to enhance efficiency and productivity. Communication and change management are also essential factors to consider when improving IT maturity. As change can be met with resistance, it is crucial to engage with stakeholders and obtain buy-in for any changes proposed. Regular communication and involvement from all levels of the organization can help ensure a smooth and successful transformation.

In conclusion, conducting IT maturity assessments is an essential tool for IT managers to achieve organizational goals and drive growth. By understanding the importance of maturity assessments, choosing the right method, and prioritizing improvement efforts, an IT manager can set their organization on a path towards success.

Chapter 35: Managing IT Security Breaches

In today's digital age, the threat of cyber attacks and security breaches looms over every organization. As an IT manager, it is your responsibility to ensure the security and integrity of your company's data and information systems. One slight vulnerability could lead to disastrous consequences, not only for the company but also for its customers and stakeholders. Therefore, it is crucial to have a solid plan in place to prevent security breaches, respond to incidents, and deal with cyber attacks effectively.

Preventing Security Breaches

The best defense against security breaches is a strong offense. It is essential to have preventive measures in place to minimize the chances of a breach occurring in the first place. This involves implementing robust security protocols, conducting regular security audits, and staying up-to-date with the latest security trends and technologies. One of the key ways to prevent security breaches is to establish a strict password policy. Enforce password complexity requirements, regularly change passwords, and implement multi-factor authentication where possible. It is also crucial to secure physical access to servers and databases to prevent unauthorized access.

Another critical aspect of preventing security breaches is educating employees about cybersecurity. Often, breaches occur due to human error, such as falling for phishing scams or using weak passwords. By training employees on best practices for data security, you can create a culture of security awareness within your organization.

Incident Response Planning

Despite our best efforts, security breaches can still occur. Therefore, it is crucial to have a well-defined incident response plan in place. This plan should include steps to be taken in the event of a breach, roles and responsibilities of team members, and escalation procedures. The first step in any incident response plan is to contain the breach. This involves isolating the affected systems to prevent further harm. Next, you must analyze the cause and extent of the breach to determine the necessary actions to mitigate it. This may involve forensics analysis, data recovery, and implementing patches or fixes.

Dealing with Cyber Attacks

In some instances, a security breach may be a result of a deliberate and malicious cyber attack. In such cases, it is crucial to know how to respond effectively to minimize damage and prevent future attacks. This may involve working with law enforcement, engaging with cybersecurity experts, and issuing public statements to reassure customers and stakeholders. It is essential to have a communication plan in place during a cyber attack. This involves communicating with employees, customers, and stakeholders to inform them of the breach and the steps being taken to address it. Transparency and timely communication are key in maintaining trust and credibility in such situations.

Going Above and Beyond

In addition to preventive measures, incident response planning, and dealing with cyber attacks, it is crucial to go above and beyond in ensuring the security of your organization's IT systems. Regularly conduct security audits and vulnerability assessments to identify and address any weaknesses in your security. Stay updated with the latest security trends and technologies, and be proactive in implementing them in your organization. Additionally, it is essential to stay informed of any security breaches or attacks that may have occurred in your industry or with organizations similar to yours. Analyze the patterns and trends to identify any potential threats and take preventive measures accordingly.

As an IT manager, it is your responsibility to ensure the security of your organization's data and IT systems. By following preventive measures, having a well-defined incident response plan, and being prepared to deal with cyber attacks, you can effectively manage and mitigate the risks of security breaches. Stay vigilant, stay educated, and stay prepared to protect your organization from harm.

Chapter 36: Managing IT Audits

The word "audit" can strike fear into the hearts of even the most seasoned IT managers. It can conjure up images of being scrutinized, criticized and ultimately, failing to meet expectations. But audits don't have to be a negative experience. In fact, they can be a valuable opportunity to evaluate and improve your IT processes, procedures and systems. In this chapter, we will explore how to prepare for audits, respond to audit findings, and implement audit recommendations in a way that will not only satisfy auditors, but also improve the effectiveness and efficiency of your IT operations.

Preparing for Audits

The best way to prepare for an audit is to always be audit-ready. This means maintaining organized and up-to-date records, implementing and adhering to policies and procedures, and regularly conducting internal audits to identify and address any potential issues. By staying on top of these tasks, you can drastically reduce the stress and workload that comes with preparing for an audit. It's also important to familiarize yourself with the audit process. Understand what the auditors are looking for, what documents they will need, and what areas they will be focusing on. This will allow you to gather and organize the necessary information in a timely manner, rather than scrambling at the last minute.

Another useful tip for preparing for an audit is to conduct a mock audit. This involves having someone from outside of your team, such as a colleague or a consultant, review your processes and procedures as if they were an auditor. This can help identify any potential gaps or issues that may need to be addressed before the official audit takes place.

Responding to Audit Findings

No matter how well-prepared you are, there is always the possibility that the auditors will find some areas that need improvement. When this happens, it's important to respond in a professional and organized manner. First and foremost, listen to the auditor's findings and ask for clarification if needed. This shows that you are taking the audit seriously and are committed to addressing any issues. Next, work with the auditor to develop a plan of action for resolving the findings. This may involve implementing new processes or procedures, providing additional documentation, or conducting further training for your team. It's also important to keep track of all communication and documentation related to the audit findings. This will not only help you stay organized, but it can also be useful if there are any disputes or misunderstandings in the future.

Implementing Audit Recommendations

After the audit is complete and the findings have been addressed, it's time to implement the audit recommendations. This can involve making changes to processes or procedures, upgrading systems or software, or providing additional training for your team. When implementing these recommendations, it's important to involve your team. Explain the reasoning behind the changes and how they will benefit the overall effectiveness and efficiency of your IT operations. This will help gain their support and cooperation in implementing the recommendations. It's also important to continuously monitor and evaluate the effectiveness of the changes. This will ensure that the recommendations were implemented correctly and are producing the desired results. Additionally, it will help identify any further areas for improvement.

In conclusion, managing IT audits may seem like a daunting task but it doesn't have to be. By being audit-ready at all times, responding professionally to audit findings, and implementing recommendations in a thorough and organized manner, you can not only pass audits with flying colors, but also improve your IT operations in the process. So instead of dreading the next audit, embrace it as an opportunity to make your IT processes and procedures even better.

Chapter 37: Managing IT Ethics and Professionalism

Understanding Ethical Issues in IT

In today's fast-paced, technology-driven world, the role of an IT manager goes beyond just managing projects and budgets. As an IT manager, you are also responsible for upholding ethical standards and promoting a culture of integrity within your team and organization. With the ever-evolving landscape of technology, it is important to understand the ethical issues that may arise in the IT industry and how to navigate them with professionalism and grace. One of the most common ethical issues in IT is the protection of sensitive data and information. As an IT manager, you are responsible for safeguarding your organization's data and ensuring that it is not misused or compromised. This includes both internal data, such as employee records, and external data from clients and customers. With the growing threat of cyber attacks and data breaches, it is imperative to stay updated on the latest security measures and regularly assess and monitor your organization's data systems.

Another ethical issue faced by IT managers is the use of personal technology in the workplace. With the rise of mobile devices and social media, employees may feel the need to use personal devices for work-related tasks, blurring the lines between personal and professional use. This can lead to potential data security risks and conflicts of interest. As an IT manager, it is important to establish and enforce clear policies regarding the use of personal technology in the workplace to avoid ethical dilemmas.

Promoting Ethical Behavior

As an IT manager, you play a critical role in promoting ethical behavior within your team and organization. You can start by setting a good example, demonstrating integrity in your actions and decision-making. Your team looks up to you for guidance and direction, and your ethical behavior will influence their own actions. It is also important to educate your team on the importance of ethical behavior in the IT industry. This includes providing training on data security and privacy, as well as emphasizing the importance of honesty and transparency in their work. Encourage an open communication culture where employees feel safe to voice any ethical concerns they may have.

Creating a code of conduct for your team and organization can also help promote ethical behavior. This code should outline the standards of behavior expected from employees and the consequences of violating these standards. By setting clear expectations, you can prevent ethical issues from arising and handle any violations in a fair and consistent manner.

Dealing with Ethical Dilemmas

Despite your best efforts, ethical dilemmas may still arise in the IT industry. These can range from conflicts of interest to issues of discrimination and harassment. It is important to address these dilemmas promptly and professionally to maintain the integrity and reputation of your organization. One approach to handling ethical dilemmas is to involve your team in the decision-making process. By soliciting their opinions and ideas, you can gain different perspectives and come up with a solution that is fair and ethical for all parties involved. It is also important to document the dilemma and the steps taken to resolve it, as it may serve as a reference for future ethical dilemmas. In severe cases, it may be necessary to seek guidance from an ethics committee or legal counsel. This is especially important in situations that may have legal implications. As an IT manager, it is important to be aware of both legal and ethical guidelines when making decisions.

In conclusion, as an IT manager, it is your responsibility to understand and address ethical issues in the IT industry. By promoting ethical behavior, you can create a culture of integrity within your team and organization. When faced with ethical dilemmas, use a collaborative approach and seek guidance when necessary. With a commitment to ethical standards, you can build a successful and trustworthy IT team.

Chapter 38: Contract Negotiations - Mastering the Art of Closing Deals

From preparing for negotiations to implementing effective negotiating techniques, the success of any IT manager largely depends on their ability to navigate and close deals. Being able to effectively manage contracts is also essential for the smooth operation of any IT organization. In this chapter, we will delve into the world of contract negotiations, exploring the strategies and techniques that can help an IT manager become a master at closing deals and managing contracts.

Preparing for Negotiations

As an IT manager, one of your key responsibilities is managing contracts with vendors, suppliers, and other external parties. This involves negotiating terms and conditions, pricing, and other provisions to ensure the best outcome for your organization. To prepare for negotiations, here are some key steps you should follow:

1. Understand What You Want

Before entering into any contract negotiation, it is crucial to have a clear understanding of what outcomes you want to achieve. This includes defining your organization's needs, budget constraints, and non-negotiable terms. Having a defined list of expectations and goals will help you stay focused during negotiations and ensure that you do not make any hasty decisions.

2. Research the Market

To negotiate effectively, you need to have a good understanding of the market and industry standards. Researching the prices and terms offered by other vendors will give you a benchmark to compare against and help you determine fair terms for your organization. This will also give you a better understanding of your bargaining power and help you make informed decisions during negotiations.

3. Know Your Negotiating Partner

While it is important to know what you want and understand the market, it is equally important to understand your negotiating partner. This includes their business objectives, their preferred negotiation style, and their strengths and weaknesses. This will help you tailor your approach to negotiations and find common ground to reach an agreement that benefits both parties.

Negotiating Techniques

Once you are well-prepared, it is time to put your negotiation skills to the test. Here are some techniques that can help you close deals and achieve the best outcome for your organization.

1. Building Rapport

Establishing trust and building rapport with your negotiating partner is crucial for a successful outcome. This involves active listening, showing empathy, and finding common ground. By building a positive relationship with your negotiating partner, you can foster a sense of cooperation and increase the likelihood of reaching a win-win agreement.

2. Focus on the Big Picture

During negotiations, it is easy to get bogged down in specific details and lose sight of the big picture. As an IT manager, it is important to have a holistic understanding of your organization's goals and priorities. This will help you focus on the key issues and avoid getting derailed by minor ones.

3. Use Effective Communication Skills

Effective communication is the key to successful negotiations. This includes being clear and concise in your communication, actively listening to your negotiating partner, and using non-verbal cues to show interest and engagement. By mastering these skills, you can ensure effective communication and avoid misunderstandings during negotiations.

Contract Management

Once you have successfully negotiated a contract, it is essential to manage it effectively to ensure a smooth relationship with the other party. Here are some tips to help you manage contracts like a pro.

1. Keep Track of Key Dates and Deadlines

One of the most crucial aspects of contract management is keeping track of important dates and deadlines. This includes renewal dates, termination dates, and any performance milestones. It is essential to have a system in place to ensure that deadlines are not missed.

2. Monitor and Review Performance

It is important to regularly monitor and review the performance of both parties to ensure that the contract is being fulfilled as agreed upon. This will also help you identify any areas for improvement and make necessary adjustments to ensure a successful partnership.

3. Build a Strong Relationship with Your Partner

A successful contract is more than just a binding agreement; it is a relationship between two parties. By building a strong relationship with your negotiating partner, you can foster open communication, trust, and cooperation, making it easier to resolve any issues that may arise during the term of the contract.

In Conclusion

Contract negotiations and management are critical skills for any IT manager. By following the above strategies and techniques, you can improve your negotiating skills and ensure that contracts are managed effectively for the benefit of your organization. Remember, successful negotiations are not about winning or losing; they are about reaching a fair and mutually beneficial agreement that contributes to the success of your business. So keep an open mind, be prepared, and use effective communication and negotiating techniques to become a master at closing deals.

Chapter 39: Managing IT for Business Innovation

In today's rapidly evolving business landscape, innovation is key to achieving success and staying ahead of the competition. As an IT manager, it is crucial to not only keep up with the latest technology trends, but also to identify opportunities for innovation and incorporate it into your IT strategy. In this chapter, we will explore the role of IT managers in driving business innovation and the best practices to effectively manage and measure its impact.

Identifying Opportunities for Innovation

Innovation is not just about developing new products or services. It can also refer to improving existing processes, systems, and strategies. As an IT manager, it is your responsibility to constantly seek out opportunities for innovation within your organization. This can involve staying up-to-date with industry trends, attending conferences and networking events, and engaging in strategic conversations with other departments. One effective way to identify potential areas for innovation is by conducting regular SWOT (Strengths, Weaknesses, Opportunities, Threats) analyses. This will help you identify any gaps or weaknesses in your current IT strategy that can be addressed through innovation. It is important to involve key stakeholders from different departments in this process to gain a diverse perspective.

Another approach is to foster a culture of innovation within your IT team. Encourage your team members to think outside the box and come up with new ideas. Incorporate brainstorming sessions and innovation challenges into your team meetings to keep the creativity flowing. By involving your team in the process, they will feel personally invested in the success of the innovation and will be more motivated to see it through.

Incorporating Innovation into IT Strategy

Once you have identified opportunities for innovation, it is time to incorporate them into your IT strategy. This involves aligning the innovation with your organization's overall goals and objectives. Innovation for the sake of innovation can be counterproductive and a waste of resources. It is important to ask yourself how this innovation will benefit the organization, improve processes, and ultimately drive business success. Incorporating innovation into your IT strategy also requires effective communication and collaboration with other departments. Often, innovative ideas may require resources or expertise from other areas of the organization. By involving other departments early on and seeking their input, you can ensure a smooth implementation and gain their support for the innovation. Another important aspect of incorporating innovation into your IT strategy is to have a well-defined plan and timeline. This will help you stay on track and ensure that the innovation does not get sidelined due to other priorities. Assign responsibilities and set clear expectations for your team to keep everyone accountable and motivated to see the innovation through to completion.

Measuring Impact

As the famous quote by Peter Drucker goes, "what gets measured, gets managed." The impact of innovation must be measured to determine its success and identify areas for improvement. There are various metrics that you can use to measure the impact of innovation, such as cost savings, increased efficiency, and customer satisfaction. It is important to set baseline metrics before implementing the innovation so that you have something to compare it to. This will help you determine if the innovation has met its objectives and if any adjustments need to be made. Regularly communicating progress and results with key stakeholders, including upper management, will also demonstrate the value of the innovation and garner support for future projects. Moreover, don't forget to recognize and celebrate the success of the innovation and the team members involved. This will not only boost team morale but also foster a culture of continuous improvement and innovation within the organization.

In conclusion, as an IT manager, you play a significant role in driving business innovation. By identifying opportunities, incorporating innovation into your IT strategy, and measuring its impact, you can lead your team towards success and help your organization stay ahead in a constantly evolving business landscape. Remember to always keep an open mind, encourage creativity and collaboration, and communicate effectively to make the most out of your innovative ideas.

www.ingramcontent.com/pod-product-compliance
Lightning Source LLC
Chambersburg PA
CBHW071300050326
40690CB00011B/2483